KINGDOM NOW... BUT NOT YET

By
TOMMY REID

Published in Buffalo, New York, by IJN Publishing and distributed by Kingdom Publishers, Atlanta, Georgia.

Most Scripture quotations are from THE NEW KING JAMES VERSION.

Printed in the United States of America.

ISBN: 0-917595-18-1

Dedicated To
Two Of My Most Respected Friends

DR. ORAL ROBERTS

Who has demonstrated his strong belief in the presentness of the Kingdom of God and its influence upon society by giving for our generation a great university, and a great medical center. This "microcosm" of Christ's Kingdom has become salt to a decaying society, and light to a darkened world.

DR. ROBERT H. SCHULLER

The warmth of the Schuller home has shown us the peace, tranquility and love for family that has truly demonstrated to us again Christ's Servant Kingdom, as evidenced in a single Christian home.

His warm and loving personality, Christian character, servant leadership, and his caring concern for hurting humanity has shown me in a single human being, the Kingdom of God in microcosm.

These two humble and loving men have shown me the true demonstration of Christ's Kingdom.

FOREWARD

It affords me personal pleasure to have the privilege of writing the foreward to Pastor Tommy Reid's book which seeks to illuminate and apply the truth of Christ and His Kingdom.

Writing is a greater task than most could imagine. Seldom can you write to please everyone and more rarely can you put into words on paper that which expresses all that you can see in the realm of the Holy Spirit.

Undoubtedly, this manuscript reveals that Pastor Reid has had an encounter with the Lord of the Kingdom. The power, truth and the urgency of the Kingdom has broken in upon him. As a writer, I could perceive the passion, as well as struggle in his person as he sought to explain the unexplainable, namely, the *mysteries* of the Kingdom!

Pastor Reid's conviction, as is mine, that you are unable to properly interpret the teachings of Jesus without first comprehending His annunciation, by word and action; His message concerning God's present authority and rulership. It is difficult to refrain from a review of the issues rather than write a foreward to the book because of the vital truths which rise to the surface in this challenging book.

A determined and resolute return to the original teachings of our Lord—who is God's ultimate standard for all truth—is most urgent for the believers of our generation. Nothing, I repeat, nothing will heal the church, strengthen the Christian's faith and restore godly influence on the earth except a proper recognition of the theoretical and practical implications of the Kingdom of God. This is effectively set forth, chapter by chapter.

The author has sought to serve us in this matter. He is a classic Pentecostal by heritage and conviction. It provides me personal reward as a Pentecostal myself, to commend this man and his message as a refreshing attempt to regain "the faith once delivered to the saints." My impression is that the author has not avoided that which is controversial, while at the same time, he writes in a conciliatory manner. He has, as well, refused to intentionally obscure issues that would affect denominational acceptance or rejection. In my judgment, the author has honestly and forthrightly set out the consequences of truth as they were discovered and formed by his own journey into God.

One clear principle that Pastor Reid has adhered to throughout the book, one most critical for sound biblical exegesis, is that the Person and the message of Jesus is the key to understanding the Old Testament and the New. While all of us may not come to the same conclusions or applications as does this book, may I commend to you, without reservation, his love for truth, his search for the real faith and above all, the primacy he gives to Christ and His Kingdom.

Read carefully, allowing the Holy Spirit to guide us in child-like simplicity that we might regain a heart obedience to the Master's command: *"Seek first the Kingdom..."*

San Rafael, California 1988 — Bob Mumford

PREFACE

"KINGDOM NOW...BUT NOT YET" is a book that had to be written. It confounds the popular stereotype of Pentecostals as people who think with their emotions rather than their minds. Great soul winners, great empire builders, yes; great theologians, no.

After reading "KINGDOM NOW...BUT NOT YET," I, as a Reformed Pastor, see the founders of Pentecostalism as men of deep theological orthodoxy and insight, who carefully avoided the popularized theological extremes of their day. Rather than accept these extremes, they adhered to the historic view of the church.

It would seem that Revival movements which rely so heavily on the inspiration of the Holy Spirit rather than the study of theology would tend to take the interpretation of the Scriptures in new theological directions. However, history proves the very opposite is true. Tommy Reid clearly establishes that the genius of true Revival is its adherence to orthodoxy, and it's linkage to the historicity of the church which precedes it. This is true specifically of the Pentecostal revival as their founding leadership dealt with the doctrines of ecclesiology, the kingdom, last day revival, and the relevancy of the teachings of Jesus.

At this point Pastor Reid takes the teaching of the presentness of the kingdom as taught by the founders of the Pentecostal movement, and develops this teaching into a worldview. Admittedly, according to the author, he goes a step beyond their development of kingdom truth, but builds his belief upon their theology, and their pre-millennial eschatology. It is interesting that the worldview developed from Pentecostal theology is nearly identical to the worldview developed from John Calvin's theology by Abraham Kuyper, in my own Reformed tradition.

"KINGDOM NOW...BUT NOT YET," with its development of a Pentecostal worldview can, "liberate" the Pentecostal movement to affect the world, as did the historic Reformers who preceded it. It is a "must" for every serious Pentecostal.

Harold Bredesen

ACKNOWLEDGMENT

Carol McLeod who has given me her time, energy, and goodwill in editing and proofreading.

CONTENTS

INTRODUCTION

Mary Jane Russell Rice had only one hour before her four daughters would return from school, and her husband, Fenton, would come home from work. She had heard of a group of people near her home in Eldred, Pennsylvania, who claimed they had received a special empowering of the Holy Spirit and were speaking in other tongues as people did in the New Testament. Intrigued by the news, and with an open heart toward God, she wondered whether this experience was really genuine.

Mary Jane and her four daughters, Ruth, Calista, Adda and Helen, were faithful attenders of the little Christian Workers Mission in the village of Eldred. The news of this "outpouring of the Spirit," as it was called, brought real hunger in her heart. With little time left between the many chores of an early 20th century mother, she noted she had slightly more than two hours left before dinner must be on the table. She paused, looked in the house, then back to the little barn situated on Elm Street in the little country community.

Suddenly she made her decision. Looking up at the hayloft in the barn, she began to talk to God, "Lord, if this strange experience I have heard about is from you, then I have only thirty minutes before I have to go in the house and begin to fix dinner. If it is from you, then I will give you these thirty minutes, and if I do not receive it in that time, then I will accept that it is not right, or at least is not right for me."

Deliberately she ascended the ladder in the layloft where she often prayed. Burying herself in the hay, she again repeated her prayer and her challenge to God. Suddenly huge waves of God's glory swept across her soul. The joy and exuberance of the Spirit of God whelmed up inside of her being, and suddenly her voice began to speak in a language she had never heard before.

The half hour was up. Now renewed in her spirit, she descended the ladder, went to her kitchen and fixed dinner for her family.

Mary Jane was my maternal grandmother, and the date was just a few years after the turn of the century, making her one of the first true Pentecostals in America. The little Gospel Mission became a Pentecostal Holiness Church, and her life the beginning of my own Pentecostal heritage.

To her youngest daughter, Helen, my mother, she conveyed her tremendous faith. And although at first Helen rejected the faith of her mother, it was in 1936, four years after my birth, and six years after Mary Jane's death, that my mother accepted Christ, along with her husband, Albert, and returned to the Pentecostal church.

That same year, they joined a small Assemblies of God church in East Aurora, New York. Now, more than fifty-two years later, I look back on more than one-half of a century of Pentecostal experience, and close association with my own denomination, the Assemblies of God.

When I was eleven years of age, my parents moved to Springfield, Missouri, to become part of the staff of Central Bible Institute, the largest Bible School in the denomination. For more than fourteen years, I lived in this headquarters city of the denomination. I was privileged to sit under the ministry of our founders, the Reverends Ernest S. Williams, Ralph M. Riggs, A. Meyer Pearlman, W.I. Evans, and my own pastor, the Rev. Thomas F. Zimmerman, who later served as general superintendent of our denomination for over twenty-five years. No one could claim being more classical Pentecostal than this writer. The very core of my theology was formed by the founders of the denomination which I serve until this very day.

It was from the founders of our denomination that I learned my theology, and all of the framework of my present thinking was shaped. To this day, I adhere to what these great men taught. The more I develop my own theology, the more I am amazed at the extent and depth of the theological insight of the founders of our church.

It is in the spirit of my strong desire to defend the faith that was delivered to me as a child, that I write this manuscript. I see us losing some of our basic theological premise upon which we built our strong belief in supernaturalism.

Therefore, I offer to the reader my heartfelt call to return to the faith of our forefathers, who prayed for the sick with a passion, as they declared the Lordship of Jesus Christ over sickness, and believed that as they conquered sickness, disease and sin in the name of Jesus Christ they were establishing the reign of Jesus Christ over the kingdom of darkness. Evangelism to these Pentecostal pioneers was the expanding of the Kingdom of God.

To these giants of faith the Kingdom of God was PRESENT, but also was TO COME. Therefore, in this manuscript we will discuss the conflict between the NOW and the NOT YET and the four areas where Pentecostals differed from Dispensationalists.

We must mention at this point, however, that the early Pentecostals accepted almost all of the eschatology of the Dispensationalists of that era. Many of our evangelists carried Dispensationalists' charts, showing the time of the rapture, the tribulation, the revelation, the final battle of Armageddon, the setting up of the Millennial Kingdom, the loosing of Satan, and the final creation of the new heavens and earth. It was on this one point where we agreed with Dispensationalism; however, in most other areas of theology, we differed dramatically.

Let us look at these areas one at a time.

Present Day Supernatural Signs and Wonders

Pentecostal historian Vinson Synan summarizes the problem as follows:

> "The fundamentalists had also been captured by a rather new Biblical view known as 'Scofieldian dispensationalism' which viewed the pentecostalist practice of glossolalia and divine healing as signs heralding the 'dispensation of grace' destined to cease with the apostles of the New Testament. The pentecostals were therefore in grave error and beyond the pale of orthodox fundamentalism" (according to the dispensationalists).[1]

I was discussing the situation with a major denominational leader recently, who confirmed my own fear of Pentecostals drifting away from their heritage as he stated that many Pentecostals today are "embracing a hermeneutic which denies their very existence."

If we are to lay the grid of the dispensational hermeneutic over the Scripture to secure a proper interpretation, we will drift further from our Pentecostal roots, and thus see less evidence of supernatural signs and wonders in our midst.

It is the humble opinion of this author that a resolution passed at the 1949 General Council, and later printed in the Pentecostal Evangel (Minutes of the General Council of the Assemblies of God, pp. 26-27), was an outgrowth of this "drift" toward embracing a dispensational hermeneutic. In defense of the General Council delegates, one must note that the resolution was a direct result of what the denomination saw as "excesses" taking place in the Latter Rain movement. However, in spite of this fact, one must note how closely this resolution aligns with the dispensational hermeneutic which stated that there was a cessation of the supernatural when the last apostle died. They further taught the cessation of the office of present day apostles and prophets. Let us examine this resolution in the light of the possibility that the grid of the dispensational hermeneutic, in fact, is being laid over the Scripture, to obtain a systematic theological rebuttal for their political dilemma.

> WHEREAS, We are grateful for the visitation of God in the past, and the evidences of His blessings upon us today, and;

WHEREAS, We recognize a hunger on the part of God's people for a spiritual refreshing and manifestation of His Holy Spirit, be it therefore;

RESOLVED, That we disapprove of those extreme teachings and practices unfounded Scripturally, which serve only to break fellowship of like precious faith and tend to confusion and division among the members of the Body of Christ, and be it hereby known that this 23rd General Council disapproves of this so called, "New Order of the Latter Rain," and to wit:

1. The overemphasis relative to imparting, identifying, bestowing, or confirming gifts by the laying on of hands and prophecy.

2. THE ERRONEOUS TEACHING THAT THE CHURCH IS BUILT UPON THE FOUNDATION OF PRESENT DAY APOSTLES AND PROPHETS (Emphasis mine).

My purpose is not to criticize the resolution, for it was certainly well-intentioned and perhaps very much needed to correct excesses, but rather to note the interesting dispensational hermeneutic used in its content. Orthodox Christian theology had continued to recognize the continued presence of the five-fold gifted ministries to the church, whereas the Dispensationalist had stated these gifted people did not exist after the death of the last Apostle. Perhaps the drafters of the resolution did not mean that apostles and prophets no longer existed, yet their wording, passed by thousands of delegates, notes an interesting mindset developing in the church.

Pentecostal Ecclesiology vs. Dispensational Ecclesiology

On one major point all Pentecostal scholars can surely agree. Early Pentecostals rejected the ecclesiology of the Dispensationalists. While the Dispensationalists believed that the church was only a substitute parenthesis, created by God after Israel rejected the Kingdom, the Pentecostalists held a much higher and more orthodox view of the church. For instance, A. Meyer Pearlman in, "Knowing the Doctrines of the Bible"[2] (1937), often designated the Christian church as the "new congregation or church" and repeatedly named Israel as the "church of Jehovah," in direct contrast to Dispensationalism, and in terms of continuing unity with Reformed Theology.

Ralph Riggs in, "Dispensational Studies" (1948), states:

> "It can be also considered that, since the giving of the covenant to Abraham, the members of this mystical church, Christ's body, have been the faith-children of the faithful Abraham."[3]

We also note that the writings of E.S. Williams carefully avoid any claim that the church belongs to a "parenthetical age." Therefore, in terms of ecclesiology, the Pentecostals always held a much higher regard for the church than their Dispensational brethren.

The Condition of the Church in the Last Days

Recently I was noting a chart in Larkin's "Dispensational Truths,"[4] in which he shows the view of the church in the Last Days as growing weaker and weaker. Apostasy abounds in the church, and this apostate condition causes a greatly weakened and eventually anemic church.

We contrast this with the Pentecostalist view, which saw both wheat and tares growing and maturing together. Though they strongly believed and preached that apostasy would abound in the church, they saw themselves as the great revival happening simultaneously in the world. They preached that God was sending the greatest revival in the history of the church to the world just before He returned.

A.G. Jeffries in "The Weekly Evangel" of March 18, 1916, writes the following glowing account of this Last Day outpouring of the Spirit:

> "The great Pentecostal revival is deepening and spreading every hour with an intensity almost inconceivable.
>
> "We have reached the limit of divine revelation. Faith has almost become sight, and revelation tangibility. God has never come nearer to men than He has the last few years.
>
> "I believe the long dark night of sin is now about past and a glorious diamond-decked morning is upon us."

This great Last Day revival was often likened in the preaching of Pentecostal pioneers to the restoration promised to Israel in the Old Testament. One of Sister Aimee Semple McPherson's sermons preached across America was from the Old Testament passage where God restored what the various insects and worms had destroyed. Whereas Dispensationalists had relegated all of these prophetic passages of restoration only to physical Israel, Pentecostal oratory constantly referred to these prophecies as having a dual meaning, restoration for physical Israel, AND restoration for the present day church. WE WERE THE PEOPLE OF THAT RESTORATION, ACCORDING TO OUR THEOLOGY.

Pentecostalism and the Kingdom of God

But most important to our study was the contrast in opinion between my Pentecostal forefathers, and the Dispensationalists in regard to the Kingdom of God. Whereas the Dispensationalist believed that the offer of the Kingdom had been withdrawn, and would not be re-offered to the world until the Millennium, Pentecostals believed in the tension between the PRESENTNESS OF THE KINGDOM, and at the same time THE FULL MANIFESTATION OF A FUTURE KINGDOM.

They expressed this strong belief in the Kingdom as they prayed for the sick, believing that as they used the name and present authority of the Name of Jesus Christ, they were enforcing the PRESENT RULE AND REIGN OF CHRIST OVER SICKNESS. They strongly linked EVANGELISM to the extension of Christ's kingdom to all of the earth.

It was, however, not only the evangelists who prayed for the sick that espoused this theological position, but the theologians of the movement as well. A. Meyer Pearlman, in his book, "Knowing the Doctrines of the Bible" (1937), makes absolutely no reference to a postponed Kingdom, but rather states with assurance:

> "That the church age IS A PHASE OF THE KINGDOM IS IMPLIED BY MATTHEW 16:18,19, by the parables in Matt. 13, and by Paul's description of Christian work as being in the sphere of God's Kingdom (Col. 4:11). Inasmuch as the 'Kingdom of Heaven' is a more comprehensive term, we may also DESCRIBE THE CHURCH AS PART OF THE KINGDOM" (emphasis mine).[5]

Ralph M. Riggs, in the "Path of Prophecy" (1937), states,

> "HE (CHRIST) ANNOUNCED THE KINGDOM (THE CHURCH) AS 'AT HAND' IN MYSTERY FORM (MATT. 4:17; 10:7; 12:28; LUKE 10:9,11; 16:16; 17:21)" (emphasis mine).[6]

Early Pentecostal preachers often referred to the preaching of Jesus concerning the Kingdom as a life-style available to us today through the empowering of the Holy Spirit, as the Spirit of God indwelt the individual believer. Whereas, the Classic Dispensationalist reserved the fullness of the manifestation of the life-style Jesus preached to a millennial reign. For instance, E.S. Williams, in "Systematic Theology" (1935), takes the position that the church and the spiritual kingdom are one and the same, with slightly different connotations. This former General Superintendent goes so far as to WARN THAT MANY DISPENSATIONALISTS:

> "take the position that the earthly ministry of Jesus was entirely Jewish, and make the Sermon on the Mount to be the laws of the Kingdom WHICH WILL BE SET UP, not church truths at all. They reason (the Dispensationalists) that THERE WERE NOT CHURCH TRUTHS EARLIER THAN THE FOUNDING OF THE CHURCH AT PENTECOST! (emphasis mine)."[7]

Therefore, my desire is to make this manuscript a defense of Classic Pentecostalism, and its belief in the orthodox truths of historic Christianity. I believe our forefathers were astute and excellent theologians. Unlike many of our theologians today, they recognized the conflict between themselves and other contemporary religious groups. They were not swayed with the popularized doctrines of the 20th century church, but held to a much more orthodox view of the Kingdom, the church, and established their view of the supernatural upon a well-accepted and orthodox hermeneutic.

Their belief, like mine today, represents a people who believed in the presentness of the Kingdom of God, as did the historic church. However, in alignment with Classic Reformed Theology, they recognized the CONFLICT BETWEEN THE NOW AND THE NOT YET.

Caught Between the Now and the Not Yet

As we begin to discuss the presentness of the Kingdom of God, may we take a look at the conflict which exists, as we are caught between the NOW and the NOT YET! In a definitive sense, we have been translated out of the kingdom of darkness, into the Kingdom of His dear Son. That Kingdom is within us, and we are subject in all areas of our life to the reign and rule of Christ. Yet in another very definitive sense, that Kingdom which exists is not yet come.

The conflict between the NOW and the NOT YET manifests itself in many ways. One would think a people who have been born into God's

Kingdom, and having theoretically learned from the teaching of the King the laws of that Kingdom, should certainly have the ability to find solutions that are full and final before Christ comes. Yet, even the most spiritual, and the most learned Christian in Kingdom truth, does not have at his disposal full and final solutions to all problems. The best of our solutions are still provisional and tentative. In fact, the very solutions themselves only point forward to Christ coming again, and with all of our knowledge and experience in the Kingdom, our solutions are always falling short of that final solution which the coming Kingdom will bring.

A warning is necessary here. The author will take a very strong view against a full establishment of the Kingdom before the physical return of Christ, for many reasons. May I, at this point, make the strongest warning I can make for my viewpoint. Emphasis on the PRESENTNESS OF THE KINGDOM, WITHOUT RECOGNITION OF THE FUTURE ASPECT OF THE KINGDOM, IS DANGEROUS. If we feel the Kingdom is fully manifested in us, and we have full knowledge of its laws and practices, we could well feel we have reached consensus as rigid as the view of the Muslim fundamentalist. We would, at that point, attempt to legislate our consensus or view of that Kingdom on everyone around us. Jesus never intended us to legislate any consensus we may come to accept, concerning His Kingdom.

The problem is that our knowledge of the Kingdom is at best incomplete, and any solutions we may find are partially flawed, tentative and incomplete. We MUST ALWAYS RECOGNIZE THE MYSTERY INVOLVED IN THE PRESENT KINGDOM. We are to live by its principles, enjoy its authority, and expand its boundaries, but recognize the very PURPOSE OF THE PRESENTNESS OF HIS KINGDOM IS TO POINT TOWARD HIS FINAL TRIUMPHANT RETURN TO THIS PLANET.

The church argues today over whether the Kingdom is present or future. EMPHATICALLY, IT IS BOTH! THERE HAS BEEN NO GOLDEN AGE IN THE PAST, AND THERE WILL BE NO GOLDEN AGE, TILL HE COMES AGAIN. However, constantly the church brings reformation and change to the world, and manifests aspects of His Kingdom to the world around it. History is replete with examples such as John Calvin and his demonstration of Christ's Kingdom in every aspect of human life in Geneva. Or one can hardly study modern church history without noting the tremendous influence Abraham Kuyper had upon the sociological structure in the Netherlands, as he taught the expansion of God's Kingdom; the Puritans that came to America with their covenant vision of God's Kingdom; or revivalist Charles Finney and his Kingdom theology, that made such an impact on America that the abolition of slavery was a direct outgrowth of his preaching.

Yet in none of these cases was the fullness of the Kingdom of God manifest, for that manifestation awaits His physical return to this planet.

Yet at the same time the tension exists, for HE DOES REIGN AND RULE TODAY. A recent article, authored by David Wilkerson, in "The Evangelist," (April 1987, p. 13, published by Jimmy Swaggart Ministries) noted the presentness of the Kingdom in these words:

> "HE IS THE KING OF GLORY! HE CAME OUT OF THE GRAVE IN FULL RESURRECTION POWER, HE ASCENDED TO HIS EVERLASTING THRONE, HE TOOK ALL POWER AND DOMINION, AND HE IS AT THIS VERY MOMENT REIGNING OVER ALL THE POWERS AND KINGDOMS OF THIS UNIVERSE (emphasis mine)."

Though some may misunderstand, this is what I am talking about. HE IS KING TODAY—that is KINGDOM NOW THEOLOGY, as this author believes it.

However, though He is King, and desires us to be the very vehicle to extend His Kingdom and dominion wherever we go, we must have the same passionate love for the coming of Christ as had our forefathers, who also believed in His present rule and reign.

So may this manuscript be what I want it to be, a call back to our roots, to our Classic Pentecostal belief in the power and authority of the triumphant church, the penetration of the Gospel of the Kingdom into all the world through a Last Day revival, and a strong belief in the supernatural.

Admittedly in this manuscript we will present aspects and implications concerning the present Kingdom of God not necessarily implied in the early teachings of my Pentecostal forefathers. However, although not necessarily implied in their writings, I believe these conclusions would be the eventual theological outcome of their beliefs. These Pentecostal pioneers came on the scene when most Evangelicals were Dispensationalists. At the same time, many liberals were preaching a gospel with social implications. This dichotomy caused my forefathers to shy away from the development of a kingdom worldview, and its attendant social implications.

However, their basic theology was certainly more Reformed than it was Dispensational. The ultimate outcome of their theology would be a

Reformed worldview, rather than the fatalistic Dispensational worldview. This manuscript attempts to show how the logical development of Classical Pentecostal theology would lead us to a worldview that causes the Gospel to have social implications as well as seeing the empowering of the Holy Spirit enabling the church to be a witness of the teaching of Jesus concerning Kingdom law and behavior.

At the same time, a wedding of orthodox kingdom truth to our pentecostal heritage would say emphatically, "EVEN SO COME QUICKLY LORD JESUS," WE LONG FOR YOUR RETURN. WE ARE A PEOPLE WHO HAVE HAD A VISION INTO THE HEAVENLIES, WE HAVE EXPERIENCED THE SUPERNATURAL, WE HAVE COME UNDER YOUR RULE AND REIGN, BUT ALTHOUGH WE HAVE EXPERIENCED THE PRESENTNESS OF YOUR KINGDOM, WE LONG FOR THAT WHICH IS NOT YET. WE ARE A PEOPLE CAUGHT BETWEEN THE NOW AND THE NOT YET!

Chapter I

A Kingdom Eschatology

"Thy kingdom come, thy will be done..."

— Jesus

Chapter I

A KINGDOM ESCHATOLOGY

I am a classic Pentecostalist. My earliest recollections of Pentecostal meetings reinforce my own belief in the Kingdom of God. I have vivid childhood memories of early evangelists consistently speaking about the power of the Kingdom when they prayed for the sick. They spoke often of the "authority of the Kingdom." When these same Pentecostal evangelists spoke of this authority, they emphatically claimed the power of the Name of Jesus over sickness, disease and all demonic activity.

However, more recently, each time the phrase "the Kingdom of God" is mentioned in Pentecostal circles, it is often equated with an a-millennial or post-millennial viewpoint. This is a misconception. The assumption is made that when one speaks of the Kingdom of God it is an expression of an eschatological viewpoint which denotes the church will completely set up the Kingdom of God on this planet.

I am a pre-millennialist who does not believe the church will completely set up the Kingdom of God on this planet until the physical return of Christ, preceded by the rapture. I do believe, however, that the church will demonstrate the power of the Kingdom and the lifestyle of the Kingdom. It is also my belief that the church will be a powerful witness to the kingdoms of this world.

I further submit that the church will raise up a standard against which the kingdoms of this world will be judged. These forceful statements of Kingdom Theology will not be established in light of modern eschatological tenets but rather by the strength of the eschatology of Jesus Himself.

Jewish Kingdom Eschatology

The dream of the Jewish Nation was to have a kingdom. Jewish theologians often look forward to a civilization where the lion would lie down with the lamb and an ultimate utopia would result from the propagation of their faith. Old Testament Prophets alluded consistently to the culture that the Messiah's Kingdom would bring, and a kingdom utopia was often defined in Jewish literature. Jewish theology was Kingdom theology.

The Jews believed that the coming of the Messiah would usher in a Kingdom where all the world would be at peace under His rulership. The men who knew Jesus as Messiah and were committed to Him in discipleship held this belief implicitly. The disciples longed for the day when their Messiah would conquer the Romans and set up a throne in the City of Jerusalem.

They further believed that their Lord would establish a Kingdom not only over Jerusalem and Palestine but over the entire world. The disciples had visions of grandeur. Two of the disciples requested that one would sit on the right hand of the throne and the other on the left. This Kingdom belief was the natural outgrowth of the Theological viewpoint of the Jewish people.

The Eschatology of the Historic Church

This Jewish Theology of the Kingdom was carried over into the early church. The Reformation further enhanced this Kingdom viewpoint.

I. John Hesselink states, "Reformed Theology is Kingdom Theology. Its concerns, like those of the Scriptures, go beyond church as well as the individual. This Biblical motif is frequently neglected or overlooked in Evangelical circles, despite the fact that the central theme of Jesus' preaching in the synoptic gospels is the coming of the Kingdom of God."[8]

Isaac Rottenburg stresses, "On one hand the Kingdom concept keeps pointing us to the future; on the other hand, that God, the Creator, is recreating the world."[9]

It is obvious as we study history that John Calvin believed that the state was a divinely appointed agency which, along with the church, was a means of establishing God's order in the world. Calvin showed concern for such mundane matters as interest rates, sewers, safety features in homes and immigration policy. He also established an academy which was to become the University of Geneva.

Calvin's goal was to manifest the Lordship of Christ in every sphere of life. In light of this, it is reasonable to assume that Reformed scholars are, in effect, Kingdom scholars.

Pentecostalism And the Kingdom

The question now arises, "But what about Pentecostalist Scholars?" Pentecostalists, although never pure Dispensationalists, were influenced greatly through the teachings of Dispensationalists such as Dr. C.I. Scofield by the use of his Notes in their Bible schools. These notes directly contradicted the Pentecostal Theologians' consistent belief in miracles, the Baptism of the Holy Spirit and the continual practice of Spiritual gifts. While Pentecostal Theologians preached miracles as a manifestation of the Kingdom of God, Dispensationalists conversely believed that the Kingdom of God was rejected by the Jews, that the

Church Age was established as a substitute for the Kingdom and that this Kingdom of God would not reappear until the millennial reign.

This philosophy was in direct disagreement with most Pentecostal Theology, which emphatically stressed the power and the authority of the Kingdom of God. Pentecostalists were in general agreement that Christ's reign was now present and that He expressed His power through the Believer's authority over sickness and disease. Therefore, like the Reformed Theologians before them, Pentecostalists were Kingdom Theologians as well.

However, possessing a Kingdom awareness does not necessarily imply that Pentecostalists, nor Reformed Theologians, believed that the church would be the agency through which the Kingdom of God would effectively subdue the planet and set up a Utopian society in the world.

The Modern Church

Today's church holds to four tenets of the millennium. In order to have a complete cognizance of a Kingdom Eschatology, it is imperative to understand these four millennial views of the Twentieth Century Church.

Pre-Millennialism

The pre-millennialist believes that the return of Christ will be preceded by the preaching of the Gospel to all nations, great apostasy, wars, famines, earthquakes, the appearance of the anti-Christ and the Great Tribulation. Furthermore, pre-millennialists believe that in the Millennial reign Christ will reign through a select group of believers and sit on a physical throne located in the City of Jerusalem.

They also believe that the Kingdom will not be established through consistent conversion of individuals across the ages, but will be established abruptly by a sudden explosion of power through the return of Christ to this planet.

Pre-millennialists believe that Jews will be converted in great numbers and that those converted will share an important rulership role in Jerusalem. Their belief continues that the ferocious beast will be tamed and evil will be held in check by Christ, the returning Messiah, through a rod of iron. Pre-millennialists maintain that rebellion will take place at the end of the 1000-year reign, which will overwhelm a number of the saints.

During this golden age, believers will live in resurrected bodies with the rest of the inhabitants of the earth who will have bodies of flesh such as we have today. Most pre-millennialists believe that after the 1000-year reign, the non-Christian dead will be resurrected and that the earth will be cleansed by fire after Satan's final loosening. Through this sequence of events the eternal status of heaven and earth will finally be established.

Post-Millennialism

The post-millennialist believes that the Kingdom of God will be extended through Christian teaching and preaching. They also believe that the world will be fully Christianized, resulting in peace and prosperity in an age called a millennium. This age will be similar to our present age. Evil, according to the post-millennialists, will not be totally eliminated but will be reduced as Christian influence increases. They maintain that the church will assume a greater role of importance in social, economic and educational fields. The millennial period will close with the second coming of Christ, the resurrection of the dead and the final judgment.

A-Millennialism

An a-millennialist believes in a continuous growth of good and evil which culminates at the second coming of Christ. At the coming of Christ the dead are raised, the last judgment is held and the Kingdom of God is established.

There is a strong emphasis by the a-millennialist that the Kingdom of God is now present in the world. It is important to note that the a-millennial view is not that there is no millennium, but that the millennium is an undetermined period of time from the Cross to the Second Coming of Christ.

The a-millennialist is certainly not a fatalist but looks forward with great anticipation to the future, which is glorious and perfect as the Kingdom of God comes on the new earth.

The Millennium and Church History

During the first three centuries of the church the pre-millennialist view pervaded. It was held by such church fathers as Papias, Irenaeus, Justin Martyr and Tertullian. During the days of Constantine, the church was given favorite status as the a-millennial view became accepted. During this period the millennium was referred to as "the reign of His saints."

The Council at Ephesus was held in the year 431 A.D. The Council condemned the belief in the millennium as superstitious. In spite of the recommendation of the Council, a pre-millennial view began to grow in the church. This view and subsequent teaching was used to strike out at the establishment itself. Leaders who claimed to be inspired by the Spirit rebelled against the oppressors in the government in the Name of God.

The Protestant Reformers decisively remained on the side of Augustine and his view of millennialism. Johanne Hienrich Alsted (1588-1638) personally revived pre-millennialism. Out of Alsted's book, "The Blessed City," published in 1627, grew the Puritan movement and finally the settlement of the United States.

Pre-millennialism then waned and post-millennialism became the prevailing eschatological position. Daniel Whitby (1638-1726) began to preach a view that the world would become converted and that the Jews would be restored to the land.

The 19th century subconsciously produced a new emphasis on pre-millennialism. The culture of this century gave birth to the French Revolution, and violent uprisings against the establishment. Conversely, the church encouraged a renewed interest in the conversion of the Jews themselves.

Dispensational Pre-Millennialism

Edward Irving (1792-1834), a stalwart member of the Church of Scotland, organized Prophecy Conferences, supported by a group known as the Plymouth Brethren. For the first time in history the coming of Christ was described in two stages. J.N. Darby, another founder of Dispensationalism, was the instigator of this tenet. He reported a view of a secret rapture after which there would be a seven-year period of tribulation which would devastate the earth. The saints would then return with Christ and they would institute the Kingdom of God upon the earth.

Such scholars as G. Campbell Morgan, H.A. Ironside, and C.I. Scofield agreed with this eschatological view. There were purposefully many basic differences between historic pre-millennialism and dispensational pre-millennialism. Dispensational pre-millennialism put emphasis on the secret rapture and the revival of temple sacrifices. This inserted an added dimension to traditional pre-millennialism. This new viewpoint contended that the Kingdom of God was not to be preached today, but rather that the Kingdom was rejected by the Jews and would not be reintroduced until Christ returned and the millennial reign was established.

In contrast, historic pre-millennialism did not reject the Kingdom of

God as being present during this age. Historic pre-millennialism fully accepts the fact that the Kingdom exists today in the hearts of believers and that the church is a living demonstration of the powerful Kingdom of God upon the earth.

Author's Tenet

All four systems of eschatological viewpoint have a certain amount of truth. This manuscript will neither accept nor reject any specific eschatological system. I define myself as a historic pre-millennialist, although I well accept many viewpoints as having facets of truth.

After years of study, research and conversation with some of the noted theological minds of this century, there are several conclusions that I believe merit consideration. They are as follows:

1. There is a covenant which binds the Old Testament and the New Testament together.
2. The Kingdom of God is central in all of human history.
3. Jesus Christ is the Lord of all history.
4. All of history is moving toward one goal—the redemption of the universe.

The Genesis Mandate—Subdue the Earth

The earth is the center of the restoration that God has foreordained. A later chapter will reinforce that the Bible begins with the premise that Satan had rebelled, was thrown out of heaven and placed upon this earth where he set up "the gates of Hell" or the "capital city of Hell." It is to this rebellion that God addressed himself in the re-creative process.

God placed man in the center of this rebellious city and proceeded to create the perfection of Utopia, or a garden, or a Kingdom, and placed man—made in God's own image—in that garden. God commanded man to tend the garden and subdue, or conquer, the earth. This is the purpose of all that God is doing on this planet. He is establishing His rule and reign over the capital city of darkness so that He may bring back to Himself *all* that have rebelled. The argument is further enhanced in the book of Colossians, Chapter 1, when Paul, the writer to the church at Colossae, states, "And by Him to reconcile all things to Himself, by Him, whether things on earth or things in heaven, having made peace; through the blood of the cross" (Colossians 1:20).

When the capital city finally falls to the authority and Lordship of

Jesus Christ, all of creation which has previously fallen to Satan will submit to the rule and reign of Christ. However, there is no indication in Scripture that there will be a conversion of Satan or his angels, but rather that they will be thrown into a place reserved for them for eternity. There is also no premise in this theology for the total redemption of all men who continue to rebel against God. They, too, will finally be deprived of their communication with God and thrown into the Lake of Fire.

The Bible, then, becomes the guidebook or the plan of restoration. Man's very purpose upon this planet is to take dominion over that which Satan has stolen from God. This begins to form a worldview of the purpose of the church and for the people of God.

Prototypes of Kingdom Rule

The Old Testament submits prototypes of God's people and the world system around them.

Israel

The first prototype is Israel, who is called of God to be a nation of priests. It was God's intent that the nation of Israel would be a people who would stand between God and the rebellious creation. These priests would represent the rebels to God and God to the rebels.

Joseph

Secondly, there is the prototype of Joseph in the land of Egypt. Joseph stood between God and a people who were coming under judgment. He would become a pseudo-saviour to them by providing a divinely-inspired way in which their sociological and economic structure would be saved through times of famine.

Daniel

Daniel is the third prototype set forth in the Old Testament. Daniel was sent as a slave to the land of Babylon and became the prime minister of that great nation. The book of Daniel states that Daniel had creative ideas or solutions for the problems of society.

All of these prototypes were obviously a demonstration of a worldview that we are to have in the midst of a rebellious society. We are to be as

Daniel and Joseph, a people that infiltrate the very fabric of our society and thus demonstrate the powers of the Kingdom of God.

The Arrival of the Second Adam

Man obviously failed through sin in his attempts to "subdue the earth for the Sovereign of the universe." Into this rebellious planet, the capital city of the kingdom of darkness, comes the only begotten Son of God, incarnate in human flesh. He was announced by his fleshly cousin John, with these words, "The Kingdom of Heaven is here!" The Kingdom of Heaven had arrived because the King of Heaven had arrived!

This King gave all authority to His disciples. He sent them out to have authority over evil of every kind. They were first to preach the Kingdom of God and then to demonstrate the power and authority of that Kingdom over the evil around them, whether that evil was manifest in leprosy, sickness, disease or even in death itself. It is profoundly interesting that in the last verse of the Book of Acts, the Scripture states that the early church went everywhere preaching those things pertaining to the "Kingdom of God" or the "reign of Christ."

The Church Pursues the Kingdom

Does this mean in all of this theological discussion that the church will set up the Kingdom of God or create a utopia upon the earth which will vanquish all evil, and where the lion shall lie down with the lamb? There are some that do believe this. The post-millennialist would believe that this kind of a Kingdom could be set up from the teaching and preaching of the church. I emphatically do not believe that the eschatology of Jesus teaches this. However, we are to be involved in the overcoming of evil with good. We must be a people who witness to the world concerning the power of the Kingdom. Our lifestyle must be a witness against the Babylonian system. On the other hand, Jesus made some major eschatological proclamations that would necessitate the belief that the church was never designed by God to completely and fully set up the Kingdom on this earth.

As previously stated, the disciples had a theory that came from their Jewish teaching. It has been established that Jewish theology was always Kingdom theology. Jewish theology taught the disciples that a Messiah would come, He would be a King, He would set up a Kingdom and banish evil from the earth.

When these young Jewish men chose to follow Jesus, they had a heartfelt belief that this Man whom they followed would, therefore, be the King. In their Jewish minds they began to devise a plan. The plan was that a gold chair would be established in Jerusalem. This Man that they followed would sit on that chair and banish the evil empire of Rome in order to set up a new Kingdom that would encompass all the earth. This Kingdom would be a utopia. Sin would be abolished and they would rule and reign with Him forever.

Jesus immediately began to change their plans for world domination. He initiated a change in their theological viewpoint that He, as a Man, would at this time set up a throne, rule the world and establish Utopia.

The Eschatology of Jesus
Wheat and Tares

As a direct contradiction to their theology, Jesus made a number of major eschatological pronouncements. The first pronouncement was that there would be a harvest and in this harvest wheat and tares would grow together for the entire duration of the harvest season. Jesus told the disciples that they would not be in a position of removing the tares, but that they would harvest the wheat. Jesus asserted that He would remove the tares Himself.

This is a major eschatological pronouncement which simply states that the disciples of Christ would never be given the opportunity to remove all evil from society. They would have to wait for the harvest. The Lord of the harvest Himself would return and complete the process by removing the tares and gathering the wheat in the barns. This destroyed their "post-millennial" viewpoint of establishing a Kingdom utopia upon the earth.

Promise of Conflict

Jesus continued to make eschatological proclamations against their viewpoint. The second was His promise of persecution. He said, "I have not come to bring peace but rather a sword" (Matthew 10:34). Again and again Jesus foretold the coming persecutions that they would suffer. These persecutions would be created by a tremendous conflict in which they would be engaged. This very conflict would be the result of the continued presence of evil in their society. The disciples were being told by Christ emphatically that neither during their lifetime nor during the lifetime of this fledgling institution called the church, would they be without persecution or conflict. This is an eschatological proclamation.

Christ is saying to His church, "You will never totally abolish evil. You will be a people that will undergo persecutions and the pressures of evil with your world."

Salt, Light and Leaven

Jesus pronounced a further eschatological proclamation when He told the disciples that they would be salt and light and leaven. Salt is the necessary preserving element in the midst of decay. The fact that they would be light indicates the very presence of darkness. Leaven is a lightening or vivifying ingredient in the bread of society. All of these identifying characteristics of the Kingdom of God on the earth are evidence that there would be an alien Kingdom within another kingdom. There would be a smaller house within a larger house.

Conflict—Continual Presence of Evil

It is my tenet that the role of the church includes conflict. Jesus predicted that the sword would even divide families. The Kingdom of God is an alien Kingdom in the midst of a kingdom of darkness. The contrasting natures of these two kingdoms co-existing on one planet produce perpetual conflict.

Occupy—Continual Presence of the Enemy

Secondly, Jesus said that we were to occupy until He comes again. Occupying is a military term that literally means to take territory. The very fact that we are taking territory means that there is territory that is yet to be possessed. There will be the continual presence of the enemy on this planet until there is a cataclysmic event that will finally abolish evil from our society.

Overcome—Continual Presence of Warfare

Thirdly, we are constantly identified in the Scriptures as overcomers. The very theme of Revelation is that "they overcame by the blood of the Lamb and by the word of their testimony" (Revelation 12:11). In the very midst of evil we are not a people being subdued but a people who are subduing. We as a people are overcomers because we are enforcing the Victory won at the cross of Christ. Kingdom theology believes in personal victory, in the corporate victory of the church, but not in universal victory until He comes again.

Continual Presence of Sickness

Jesus told the disciples that they were to heal the sick. This would imply that we live in a world which will continually be embattled by sickness. If there did not need to be a healing from sickness then there would not be the presence of sickness. Jesus never indicated that the church would eradicate sickness, but rather that it would be a teacher of healing in a sick world. This, too, is an eschatological proclamation.

The Falling Away

II Thessalonians 2:3 predicts a desertion from among the ranks. Often the Scripture alludes to the apostasy, or the falling away. There cannot be a falling away unless there is evil which instigates that falling away. One would hardly yield to temptation unless temptation was present. One would hardly fall away from the ranks or become apostate if there were not a conflicting force pulling. Therefore, it is my firm belief that evil will continue to exist in our society until the physical return of Christ.

The Role of the Church

What is the role of the church, if it is not to completely establish the Kingdom of God? I believe that the role of the church is threefold. First of all, the role of the church is to enforce the past victory which Christ won on the cross. Secondly, it is to be a witness to the kingdoms of this world and to be a witness against the world system. Thirdly, the role of the church is to be involved in and to penetrate the spheres of our society with the teachings and the demonstration of the Kingdom of God.

"Eschaton" is the Greek word which defines the phrase "last days" as found in Hebrews 1:2. That Scripture says, "In these last days (eschaton) God hath revealed Himself." The Book of Acts and the Book of Joel state, "I will pour out my Spirit in the last days (eschaton)." The last days, therefore, are not just simply the ten years before the physical return of Christ, but rather it is a period of time beginning with the Incarnation and ending with the triumphant return of Christ.

During the forepart of the last days Jesus conquered hell and death by taking the keys. The Scripture further states that the prince of this world *is* or *was* judged. We are given the power to enforce a victory Christ has already won. I believe that the purpose of the church is to occupy, or to enforce that.

The last days are also predicted to be an intensification of evil. There is prophesied an apostasy, but also a great spiritual renewal. The Scripture indicates the maturing of wheat and tares. The increasing influence of salt, light and leaven is also implied.

There is one event that has greatly confused the church when considering the plan of the Kingdom. This event, the church has recently defined as the "rapture." The word "rapture" is never used in Scripture. It is a term that Bible scholars have used to define that event so beautifully described in I Thessalonians. The rapture is simply that time when Christ shall come near to the earth and the dead in Christ shall rise first and we that are alive and remain shall be caught up with Him and be changed from mortality to immortality.

Some Bible scholars view the major purpose of the rapture as a catching away of the saints before the great tribulation. Though this may be true, this is *not* the theological purpose of that event. This event has a much deeper spiritual meaning. It is vital to understand *what* transpires in the rapture, in order to understand *why* the rapture transpires.

Scripture indicates that we are going to be changed from mortality to immortality. Both the dead in Christ who will be restored to their resurrection bodies, and we who are alive and remain, shall be changed into an immortal body. At that point in history, the last enemy of man shall be overcome, the enemy known as death. From that moment into all eternity the church will never again know any kind of defeat. There is nothing that will be able to defeat her, for as a church, she shall be absolutely immortal.

The purpose of obtaining this immortal body is to become an unconquerable foe. In the ancient Jewish bridal ceremony, the bride herself would go out to meet the bridegroom, be united with him outside of the house and then return with him. This is also true in the coming scenario of eternal history. The church will be caught up with Him. We, His bride, shall go out to meet Him for the purpose of becoming the church immortal, and then return with Him in glory.

As we return on our white horses, following Christ on His white horse, the battle of Armageddon will be fought and the Kingdom of God will finally be set up upon the earth.

The Kingdom cannot be set up fully upon the earth until the church reaches the state of immortality so that they can never again be conquered. The church can never set up the Kingdom of God without the physical presence of Christ returning with them, as Head of the church, to set up His Kingdom. It is the church who will return with Christ. It is the church who will ride their conquering white horses with Him. It is the church who will fight in the final battle of Armageddon and thus establish the total rule of Jesus upon this planet.

It will be during the final battle of Armageddon that all of the forces which have been evil shall fall. Jesus Christ and His church will win the victory and set up His Kingdom upon the planet. The result of that final victory will be the reconciliation of the entire universe to the Lordship of Jesus Christ.

Author's Tenet

Therefore, I submit to you in this first chapter, that I have chosen to be a pre-millennialist. The church was never set up by Christ to be the total conqueror of the planet. We are to remain a people who will be persecuted and, therefore, will confront evil. We are a people who will be salt, light and leaven only, and never the whole loaf. We are a people who will be men and women with a sword and we will undergo persecution.

But there is coming a glorious day when the Kingdom of God will be fully set up. You and I will play a vital part in that final battle. However, even now, the Kingdom of God is here present in us, and we are to be a people who enforce His victory on this planet and look forward to the final battle when all shall be accomplished.

Chapter II

The Kingdom And The Contemporary Prophetic Voice

"God will have the last word and it will be good!"

— Robert Schuller

Chapter II

THE KINGDOM AND THE CONTEMPORARY PROPHETIC VOICE

I have truly enjoyed the last move of the Holy Spirit that God sent to His church. I have enthusiastically welcomed the great influx of people that have come into the church from the Charismatic movement and from the Jesus movement. It has been with great eagerness that I have anticipated what God was going to do next in His church.

About six or seven years ago, after the Charismatic Renewal had somewhat waned, God spoke to my heart about the future of the Church. He said to me, "As the last move of the Holy Spirit affected the church, the next move of the Holy Spirit will affect society. There will be a healing of the land." As I pondered this message that I believed to be from the Lord, I again heard his voice saying, "The next truth that I will emphasize to my Body will be an understanding of the Kingdom of God."

A Revolutionary Vision

My life had been literally transformed several years earlier by a vision which was described in my book, "The Exploding Church."[10] At that time I had prayed, "Lord, show me the world as You see it." As that prayer reiterated itself from my spirit, I developed a great hunger for a revelation from the Holy Spirit. God satisfied this hunger in a most unusual way.

One day as I was driving toward the City of Buffalo, onto the Seneca Street ramp from the New York State Thruway, the highway in front of me suddenly disappeared and I began to see the world before me as if I were an astronaut. I watched the world as it turned and I saw North America and then South America. I saw the continents of Africa and India pass before me and the great oceans which separated the masses of land.

Suddenly, I saw two nail-scarred hands coming toward the world. My first reaction was that these were hands of judgment and that God was going to destroy the world in one great catastrophic act of judgment. Instead, those Hands lovingly embraced the world and gently caressed the planet.

I then saw these nail-scarred hands of Jesus with mercy and compassion open the world so that I could peer inside. In the depths of this gigantic ball of matter that we call "Earth," I saw a broken heart. My life and my theology were transformed that day while traveling from the Thruway to Seneca Street. I had preached the judgment of the world for many years, and suddenly, I saw the Love of God for the world.

Now, ten years later, this new revelation of the Kingdom of God that was being birthed in my spirit began to transform my heart as did that first vision. I knew in my spirit that I was going to begin to find in Scripture the relationship of God's Kingdom to the world itself.

As I meditated on these thoughts, I began to envision what the Kingdom of God had to do with its relationship to the earth. God said that He would destroy those that destroy the earth (Revelation 11:18). Jesus said in Matthew 5 that the meek would inherit the earth. Abraham, in the Book of Romans, was identified as "heir of the world." What, I wondered, was God saying to me? How was He going to reveal to me the Kingdom of God?

A Kingdom Journey

Over the past few years I have gone on a personal spiritual journey, searching the Scriptures to find out exactly what is the meaning, purpose and identity of the Kingdom of God. Through this journey I have come to the conclusion that God is saying several things to the Church.

First of all, God is revealing that the reign of Christ is *now*. He is emphatically repeating that Jesus Christ is the Lord of history. God is reiterating that Satan has been defeated historically and as the prince of this world has been judged (John 16:11). I have learned to relate all of the victories that we accomplish as the Church to what Christ has already accomplished on the cross of Calvary two thousand years ago. I have also come to the conclusion that the maturing of the church will come as we make practical the "reign of Christ" in our individual lives.

It is not an outward manifestation of holiness that we need in the church, but rather an outworking of that which has already been accomplished inwardly. Christ has not only taken up residence in our lives, but He has made His Lordship known and His reign in us is *now*.

Secondly, the coming renewal that God desires to give to the Church will come with the proclamation and the demonstration of the Gospel to *all* the world. The knowledge of the Word of God will fill all the earth (Isaiah 11:9). That is not only a knowledge of the Book, but also a knowledge of the active Word as lived through the people of God. This knowledge will be learned not only by proclamation but especially by the demonstration of the Kingdom of God to the world.

Thirdly, I believe that as we learn of the Kingdom of God we will infiltrate the very fabric of our society. We will become salt and light and leaven. We will become that city on the hill to a world that's lost, dying and hurting. We are to become a Daniel people, with power to change the world.

Finally, I have found the Bible to be my handbook of responsibility. The Bible is my training manual as to what my responses should be to the sociological, ecological and economic ills of the world.

As Daniel found creative answers to the problems of his society, I believe a full revelation of God's Kingdom will bring healing to the land in which we live. But as I ponder what God is doing in and through the church in this present day, I go back in history to see that our church fathers, since the days of the Reformation, have been concerned about the church manifesting the Kingdom of God to the earth and thus becoming a healer of the land. From John Calvin to the late A.A. van Ruler, there has been a beautiful blending of a robust, individual piety with a very practical concern for involvement in the world. Calvin saw the government as a divinely-appointed agency which, along with the church, was the way that God would establish His order in the world.

Christian leaders, throughout history, have been carrying a "cultural" mandate to the world. There has always been in Reformed Theology an emphasis on Christ the transformer of culture, rather than Christ being anti-culture. Theologians have encouraged the Body of Christ to maintain a vision of "holy worldliness."

And so, as I took my personal journey into the study of the Kingdom of God in the world, I began to note the healing of the land would begin to be performed as the church begins to demonstrate the teaching of the Kingdom of God to the world. I thrilled as I read that story of the beloved benefactor of the modern church, John Calvin, as he went to Geneva to "establish the Kingdom of God in a decadent society."

Dietrich Bonhoeffer

Dietrich Bonhoeffer, one of the great preachers of the World War II era, gave a prophetic word concerning the future of the church and its effect upon society, while imprisoned in a Nazi war camp.

In a book entitled "Essays of Understanding," edited by A.T. Clawson[11], Harvey Cox writes about the Bonhoeffer legacy. In this, Cox identifies four areas in the personality of the Bonhoeffer writings which he defines as the Bonhoeffer legacy. Mr. Cox states that Bonhoeffer called for an enlargement of the ecumenical parameter in which the Body of Christ would express its unity.

Secondly, Bonhoeffer went on to outline the tactics for determining concrete and specific political involvement of the church. This involvement would evolve as the Church recognized the cultural mandate that the people of the Kingdom of God are biblically implored to make to their world. Thirdly, Bonhoeffer states the need for the church to explore new forms of structure and church life. Lastly, Bonhoeffer predicted a delineation of a non-religious hermeneutic commensurate with tradition and modern life.

Mr. Cox states that the trend of Bonhoeffer's thinking might conclude that an appropriate outcome of the Bonhoeffer legacy would, in reality, become the re-Judaizing of Christianity and its challenge would be fourfold. First, the adjustment concerning the notions of man, his nature, his possibilities and his capabilities. Bonhoeffer indicated that this adjustment may demand a complete reversal of the Augustinian development. This would require a re-establishment of a Judeo-Christian anthropology as opposed to the Greek anthropology developed in the church as a result of Gnosticism and Asceticism brought into Christian thinking through such men as Thomas Aquinas.

Secondly, "prophet" Bonhoeffer went on to state that the future of the church would indicate that we must have a diminution of the importance of theology itself. Thirdly, the need to develop a radical Christianity that would define what Christ is today and how He relates to our world. Fourthly and finally, Bonhoeffer predicted an appropriation of the ethical character of Jewish thought, described by Abraham Hirschel as the wonder of doing and the divinity of deeds.

I quote from the writings of Bonhoeffer:

> "It is said that the distinctive feature of Christianity is the proclamation of resurrection hope, and this means the establishment of a genuine religion of salvation, in the sense of release from this world. The emphasis falls upon the boundary drawn by death. But this seems to me to be just the mistake and the danger. Salvation means salvation from cares and need, from fears and longing, from sin and death into a better world beyond the grave. But is this the distinctive feature of Christianity as proclaimed by the Gospels and St. Paul? I am sure it is not. The difference between the Christian hope of resurrection and a mythological hope is that the Christian hope sends a man back into his life on earth in a wholly new way which is even more sharply defined than it is in the Old Testament."[12]

God is giving a new mandate to the church through the voice of the prophets, whether they be Calvin or Bonhoeffer or men that speak singly from the heart of God.

Rifkin, in his dynamic book, "The Emerging Order," states that the evangelical church is "redefining our role in society according to the mandate of Genesis Chapter 1." Rifkin continues that this will be a "new reformation with greater consequences than that of Martin Luther."[13]

Prophets still speak to the church today. I believe that Bonhoeffer was prophetic when he stated his profound proclamations from the Nazi concentration camp. I believe that the church must listen and redefine the magnificent Kingdom of God and the effect that it is to have upon the world.

Chapter III

The Kingdom And Revival Movements

"He who shall introduce into public affairs the principles of primitive Christianity, will revolutionize the world."

— Benjamin Franklin

Chapter III

THE KINGDOM AND REVIVAL MOVEMENTS

"If my people, which are called by My Name, shall humble themselves and pray,...then will I hear from heaven and heal their land" (II Chronicles 7:14). The Scripture places a great emphasis on healing. This is because man has severe hurts due to the injustice which society has brought to bear upon the inhabitants of the earth. As in the Book of Chronicles, revival is always God's answer to the hurts of man which man endures because of the injustices which sinful society has imposed upon him.

Old Testament Revivals

At least several great revivals took place in the Old Testament. They were: the revival under Asa in II Chronicles 15, the revival under Jehoash in II Kings ll, the revival under Hezekiah in II Kings 18 and II Chronicles 29, the revival under Josiah in II Kings 22 and II Chronicles 34 and 35, the revival under Zerubbabel in Ezra 5 and 6, and finally, the revival under Nehemiah in Nehemiah 9 and 12.

These Old Testament revivals were marked by several major characteristics. First, they each occurred in a day of moral darkness and national depression. The national depression was partially caused by a severe economic recession or depression. Each of these revivals began in the heart of a prophet or a single man of God. Each of these revivals rested basically on the teachings and the propagation of God's Word and was a result of preaching and proclaiming the Word of God. Each of these revivals resulted in a return to the worship of God and a destruction of idolatry.

Every revival in the Old Testament also included a separation from the sinful behavior that was evidenced in the society before a time of national repentance. Every Old Testament revival reemphasized blood sacrifice and brought a restoration of tremendous joy and gladness in the church. All Old Testament revivals were followed by a time of national prosperity and a return to a positive economic climate.

Upon studying the characteristics of Old Testament revivals, a pattern begins to establish itself. One motif in this Old Testament revival pattern is that a healing of the land was always associated with revival. The Kingdom of God always brings tremendous sociological healing to a society which has been sinfully decadent and then returns to God.

Early Church Revivals

The revivals that captured the attention of the New Testament and early church also merit study as we pray for God to send a revival today.

The first is the revival under St. Francis of Assisi (1182-1226). St. Francis was an ex-soldier and playboy, who started with merely twelve disciples. By the time of his death, his message had become so powerful that his disciples numbered into the thousands.

The great revival whose motivating voice was a prophet by the name of Savonarola (1452-1498) also had a profound influence on the early church. Savonarola's preaching included a prophetic word of judgment for a very corrupt generation. He is often referred to as the John the Baptist of his time. Historians say that his sermons were full of fire and searing conviction. One of the historians says that people paled, trembled, and their eyes glazed with terror as tears gushed from their eyes. His hearers would beat their breasts and cry to God for mercy.

Another historian says the mere sound of Savonarola's voice was like a clap of doom that would cause a cold shiver to run through the marrow of your bones. He so transformed the society of the city of Florence that even today engraved over the town hall of Florence, Italy, are the powerful words, "Jesus Christ is King." The church tragically ended Savonarola's life by hanging him. Society had accepted his reformation, but the church had not.

The Reformers

The Reformers of the 16th century were the next group of prophets that brought a sweeping revival to the Church. Among the ranks of these history-changing men are Luther, Zwingli and Calvin. They brought tremendous change to the world in the form of sociological reformation. Much of our Western civilization has been built on the content of their preaching. Freedom, authority and sovereignty were the three basic considerations of the Reformers' messages.

The Reformers preached freedom as they emphasized their message of justification by faith rather than by works. They talked of authority as they expressed the Lordship of Christ over all things. They taught of the sovereignty of God which would influence and change the society in which they lived.

The 1700's was a century of darkness and gratifications of the flesh. A reformation was desperately needed in the sociological structure of the day. Society had thrown off all of its restraints and plunged into drunkenness and immorality. History reports that every sixth house was a gin-stop. People were extremely cruel and inhumane to one another. The great sport of the day was to go to the town square and watch as people were hanged for alleged crimes. These hangings were watched by thousands, who brought their children with them and fought for the best view. Prisons were nightmares and toilets were open sewer trenches. Into this decadent sociological malaise came the great John Wesley, and with John Wesley came the Great Awakening.

John Wesley

John Wesley (1703-1791) trained hundreds of preachers. He preached for sixty-five years and literally changed the sociological structure of his world. Among the 233 books which John Wesley authored were included a book on health remedies and one of the earliest texts on electricity. Fifty of his volumes were on theology. John Wesley was interested not only in religion but on the whole sphere of a man's life. John Wesley had a tremendous interest in the reformation of society and the healing of the land.

George Whitefield

John Wesley won a young man to Christ by the name of George Whitefield (1714-1770). Whitefield's parents ran a tavern where the pimps plied their trade. He loved novels and plays and was a great actor. Whitefield was 21 years old when he preached his first sermon. An entire nation was startled by the voice of this fledgling prophet. The established church finally closed the door to the preaching of Whitefield, as it had to many of the other prophets and evangelists of the day. Undaunted, Whitefield began to preach to the miners. Crowds of up to thirty thousand people came to hear him preach. White gutters would form on their coal-blackened cheeks as tears rolled down from their eyes.

Although Whitefield was an early convert of John Wesley's, later in life they became theological opposites. In spite of theological differences, they remained friends. When Whitefield was asked if he would see Wesley in heaven, he replied, "I fear not, for he will be so near the throne and we at such a distance that we shall hardly get a sight of him." Whitefield ministered to the disenfranchised of his day and made a major sociological statement in doing so. Whitefield was concerned that the land would be healed.

Charles G. Finney

Charles G. Finney (1792-1875) is the cornerstone of our historical look at revivals. He was not only a revivalist but also a sociological reformer. Before his conversion in 1821, Finney was a musician, a mocking pagan, an expert marksman, a sailor and an athlete. This worldly man was marvelously converted and received what he defined as the Baptism of the Holy Spirit. Eighty per cent of his converts remained in the church. He is defined by historians as "the most impressive revolutionary that America has ever produced."

When Charles Finney became prominent on the American religious scene, the hallmark of the business community was economic gain with injustice to the poor. Gambling and greed were evidenced everywhere and riches were in the hands of only a few. There was a "playboy" philosophy and immorality ruled the land. It was a day of commercial corruption, but, most of all, a day of political corruption. This day will always be remembered for one of the worst atrocities ever known to mankind—the inhumanity of slavery. The religion of the day was not traditional Christianity but simply atheism.

Although Charles Finney brought revival to many cities, transformed the church and won many to Christ, it is the reformation of society for which Finney will be most remembered. He addressed America's great abomination—slavery—with a passion.

Africa had been raped and over one hundred million men and women had been carried away as slaves. During the transition from Africa to America, only ten million black Africans survived. The defenders of slavery claimed it was a Christian institution because it brought heathen Africans to a Christian civilization. Finney added that America was neither Christian nor civilized.

The 1857 revival led by the evangelist Finney was so deeply to affect the destiny of the United States that the revival-created sentiments would put Abraham Lincoln into the office of the Presidency.

Gilbert Barnes, in his study of the real roots of the anti-slavery movement, proved the true cause of anti-slavery was the religious faith of individuals, the moral ideas of heroes and the dedicated efforts of a handful of determined men who were called a "holy band." It was this reformation attitude that was formed out of the meetings of Charles G. Finney. Finney preached that converts did not escape from life, but that they began a new life in the interest of God's Kingdom with no separate interests. He founded the "holy band." The "holy band" was a crusade against slavery and was the direct result of the revival convictions and conversions through the ministry of Charles Finney. It led to the formation of abolition societies, a religious crusade against slavery, and finally, as stated, the election of Abraham Lincoln.

Covenant Vision

It can be noted that all earlier revivalists and reformers were united in their belief that Jesus Christ held the divine rights to the deeds of society and all of its institutions. It was, and still is, God's will to bring back fallen, decadent structures under the Lordship of Jesus Christ. It is the duty and mandate of the church to bring all things under the Lordship of Jesus Christ.

It is said that John Wesley's Methodists did more to save England from the bloodbath that took place in France than any other force.

Every revivalist of the past, until about 1850, linked conversion and spiritual growth directly to the changing of society. These revivalists had a grand and glorious covenant vision of a mighty revival that would spread throughout the world. The purpose of this visionary revival was to prepare mankind for the coming of Christ, who would return and set up His millennial Kingdom.

One cannot study the history of either Old Testament or New Testament revival without directly linking the alteration and healing of society to what God was doing in the land. This does not necessarily indicate that the Kingdom of God was totally set up in any revival of the past, nor will it be totally set up in any revival of the future. It does indicate that much of the hurts of the human race are a direct result of the sin of nations and of people. And when people turn from their sin, they also turn from hurting other people. When we turn from hurting other people, society is healed, which brings healing to the land.

It is a Scriptural mandate for Christians to fall to their knees and to pray for the healing of their land. God desires all Christians to develop the worldview that will bring healing to humanity.

When the Kingdom of God is combined with revival, a powerful force is set into motion. When the reign of Christ is truly present in my life and in the life of the corporate church, there is a power that will bring reformation and healing to the land. This healing will be so complete that the people of the land will no longer hurt.

A revival-Kingdom mentality is needed in the church today just as it was needed when God raised up a John Wesley and a Charles Finney. The church must recognize the mandate of the Kingdom of God to penetrate the very aspects of society that make people hurt.

Chapter IV

The Kingdom And Its Effect Upon The World System

"The best theology is rather a divine life than a divine knowledge."

— Jeremy Taylor

Chapter IV

THE KINGDOM AND ITS EFFECT UPON THE WORLD SYSTEM

The Kingdom of God, when presented and demonstrated in a practical, life-changing manner, will have a powerful effect upon the world system of the day. This is our Biblical mandate, to form a theology in which we recognize the ability of the church to have a profound influence upon the society in which it abides.

Jeremy Rifkin, in his book, "The Emerging Order," states:

> "A major reformulation of Protestant doctrine is beginning to take shape. At its center is the story of creation from the Book of Genesis. This reformulation could set the stage for a third great awakening in America and a new covenant vision for a steady-state economy. Not surprisingly, the theologians who are refocusing on the story of creation and redefining its central message are largely unaware of the profound revolutionary effect their theories could have upon America and the world. Nonetheless, their reconstruction of doctrine continues to ripple out into wider circles. If it becomes a tidal wave within the Christian community, then Luther and Calvin may well be retired to the theological archives to be replaced by the yet-unnamed heretics of a second-grade reformation."[14]

In the last days of the 20th Century Church, pastors from all denominations, especially those in circles which emphasize the Holy Spirit, are dealing with their own reinterpretation of the Word of God in the light of the Kingdom of God. These new evangelical reformers are seeking out truth, and many of them return to the first chapters of Scripture to see God set the stage for what He will do in "reclaiming the earth for the King."

The Garden of Eden

God commanded man not only to tend the garden but also to subdue the earth. This brings forth an interesting question. Did God create man to bring the earth back under the structure of His rule and reign as man became God's agent for reclamation of the rebel and cursed earth?

Is it possible that when God accomplished His purpose in creation from a mass that was without form and void that He concentrated on one localized spot called the Garden of Eden? In Eden the reign of God was complete and perfect. There was peace in the Garden and a divine Utopia. Here was the model millennial Kingdom. Perhaps God's very purpose was that man was to become the agent through which He was to extend the reign of God to all the earth. This may well be the very meaning of "subdue" the earth.

If this is true, it presupposes that the Bible is the handbook for man's dominion over the earth. A systematic theology of dominion over the earth would then result from a study of the total context of Scripture.

The House of God

Scripture many times refers to the earth and the heavens as the "habitation of God." David said, "The earth is the Lord's and the fullness thereof" (Psalm 24:1). David further proclaims, "The heavens declare the glory of God" (Psalm 19:1). It is, therefore, reasonable to assume that the universe itself, in its totality, is the habitation of God. It is *His house*. Psalm 36 is a beautiful exposition of the world that God has made. The Psalmist talks about the heavens and the stars, the mountains and the rivers. It is in this context that the Psalmist David prophesies that the people of God "feast on the abundance of Your house" (Psalm 36:8). Therefore, the first "house" of the Lord is the visible universe. This larger "house" has been disordered by Satan.

The Bible goes on to describe a "smaller house" or a "house within a house" or the "Tabernacle of God." In the Old Testament, the Hebrew word was "beth," which also means family. In the New Testament, that house or Tabernacle of God is the Church. This "house within a house" is defined in Psalm 36:5-9 and in Exodus 25:8 as the place where God would place His presence. His presence would turn a wilderness tent into a divine sanctuary. His presence turns a stone temple into the dwelling place of God. His presence transforms a scattered people into God's house. A physical cosmos becomes God's house through the creative power of God's presence. It is God's physical and spiritual presence that makes the difference and brings order out of chaos.

The "larger house" is, then, all of the created universe into which Satan has brought disorder. The "smaller house," or God's present Eden, is the prototype, the model community, in which there is Divine order. Due to God's presence in the "smaller house" it becomes a model to the greater house of the governmental reign of God. Thus, Eden was a prototypical community, as is the church today.

Secondly, Israel was to be "a nation of Priests" and, therefore, was the prototypical community to model the reign of God to the world.

Thirdly, Jesus came as a human being in whom dwelt the presence of God and, therefore, became as a person, the "prototypical community."

Fourthly, as Christ leaves the world, He empowers His disciples and indicates that they receive His presence in them. Then they, too, become that prototypical community, or God's present Eden, to both proclaim and to demonstrate the reign of God upon the earth.

Thus, the purpose of the community of God is not just to get men into the church but for the church to get the Kingdom of God that is within them into the world.

Israel failed to understand this. They assumed that God had called them to become "His favored sons." In reality, they were defined as the people in whose midst God dwelt. They were to be priests to the rest of the world. Abraham's seed was to bless all the nations of the world, rather than merely being blessed by God themselves, as a result of their obedience to God's law.

Evangelicals in the Kingdom

Recently, Evangelicals have written a number of books concerning moral, social and political issues. However, as Robert E. Webber, in his book, "The Secular Saint," stated, "Evangelicals are still confused about how they are to be responsible Christians in the world."[15]

Evangelicals gathered and discussed their responsibility to society in 1973. The result of that historic meeting was the writing of "The Chicago Declaration." The very purpose of this document was to be a vehicle for the awakening of a slumbering evangelical social conscience.

Our evangelical problem lies in the fact that we are Evangelicals. An Evangelical requires that his entire life and belief system be founded on the Word of God. Our theology is centered on Christ as the Saviour who forgives sin. Our preaching has largely revolved around this one major theme. As revivalists, we emphasize the saving power of Christ and God's judgment upon the sinner who will not repent. The Charismatics among us have further preached the healing power of Christ. However, neither our Christology or our entire contextual theology has given us the basis for a cultural mandate to our world.

I believe that this will be the very essence of the next reformation of the church. The Bible must become more than a handbook of "personal salvation." It must become a mandate for the reestablishment of Christ's rule and reign over the earth and the rebellious portion of the universe over which Satan now asserts dominion.

This is the very purpose of the prayer of Christ in John 17, as He asks the Father that He not take them out of the world, but keep them "from the evil in the world." We must view the entire Scripture as the handbook for our relationship to the world, and the influence that it mandates God's people are to be to the kingdoms of this world. We are to be as Joseph was in Egypt, a saviour to the society of his day. We are to be as Daniel was to Babylon, the creative power with the solutions to difficult problems. We are to be, as Christ commissioned us to be—salt, light and leaven to the hurting world.

We are to be that "house within a house." The Bible must become God's mandate to bring justice into a hurting society of our world. As Rifkin states, "God's very first commandment to humankind in the book of Genesis is being redefined. Its redefinition changes the entire relationship of human beings to God and the temporal world."[16] We need to take an intensive look at the very foundation of the Scripture and its command for man, made in the image of God, to "subdue the earth."

To do so, we must reexamine the fact that Jesus gave His disciples "power" or "dominion" over the power of Satan. Did Jesus do this simply so they would heal a few isolated bodies, or was that a continued Divine mandate in the entire context of Scripture? Are we to be the subduers of the earth? Why did Jesus tell us that the "gates (government) of hell (kingdom of darkness) shall not prevail against it (us)" (Matthew 16:18)? Do we not today have a Genesis mandate, an entire Biblical mandate, to subdue and to be the aggressive occupying force that will subdue the earth?

Pat Robertson stated in a recent interview in the BUFFALO NEWS, "The church is moving from a millennial viewpoint to a Kingdom-now philosophy." This dynamic founder of the CBN network, in his book, "The Secret Kingdom,"[17] challenges the Christians of America to develop a Kingdom mentality that will create Christian servants who will serve, and through their service bring productive change to our social structure.

Jeremy Rifkin further states, in his provocative book, "The Emerging Order," that, "At this very moment, a spectacular change in Christian theology is taking place virtually unnoticed. The change itself is simple but basic. The ramifications are extraordinary. God's very first commandment to humankind in the book of Genesis is being redefined. Its redefinition changes the entire relationship of human beings to both God and the temporal world."[18]

Rifkin's "unnoticed" has become increasingly noticed. We can hardly have a Moral Majority among us without developing a theology of responsibility for social change. It is obvious the greatest single cultural force in American life today is the Evangelical/neo-Pentecostal community.

But then, we ask the question, "Why have we not, as Evangelicals, developed a theology for social reformation?" Perhaps a look at our recent history will answer that question.

Our fatalistic view of the world has been shaped by an emphasis on the escape of the church from the earth's problems, through rapture. This has created an unbalanced view of the responsibility of the church to sociological reformation. The eschatological position is inconsequential to a theology of responsibility as long as we do not permit the overriding philosophical position of our eschatology to shape and form our view of the church, its power, purpose and responsibility for social reformation.

Every revival until approximately 1860 brought great sociological reformation to the world. The question remains, "Did the theological development of a new dispensational pre-millennial view and its attending fatalistic philosophy of escapism alter the social mandate of the church and its effect upon the world?" This is not a treatise concerning the rights and wrongs of any eschatological viewpoint. Therefore, the dispensationalist viewpoint is not rejected, but rather, the subsequent philosophical fatalism that developed through a people whose emphasis was on leaving the world rather than changing the world. It is possible to hold a strong view of the physical return of Christ in an event called the "rapture" without so emphasizing the centrality of a future event over and above the centrality of the Cross as the point at which God purchased the redemption of the world.

Our fatalism also has been formed through our modern emphasis on science. The rather recent discovery of the Law of Thermodynamics has shaped our philosophical view of the world. The Second Law of Thermodynamics states that all matter and energy was created in this original state with an order and value to them. That ordered state is continually being eroded by an irreversible natural process. According to this Law of Entropy, all matter and energy are constantly and without exception moving from an ordered to a disordered state. It seems that this fatalistic view of matter has also infiltrated our fatalistic view of society. Evangelicals have basically embraced this seemingly scientific view of the earth and society and its attending fatalism.

Many Evangelicals spiritually grew up within the confines of a small, anemic, minority church that was largely impotent in the ability to bring sociological change to the world. Now, we have awakened to a world in which we have the power, prestige, and ability to bring sociological change.

We are reexamining our theology of fatalism because of our ability to bring this change. Therefore, it is vital that we develop a theology of sociological responsibility. If this does not occur, we will again permit the liberals and the liberation theologians to shape our world, while we go merrily along awaiting the rapture. May we not find ourselves where the church in Russia found themselves, "arguing about the color of the drapes in the Cathedral while the atheists were building a newly-reformed society in Russia"?

The Church of Jesus Christ today desperately needs to follow the prophetic advice of Dietrich Bonhoeffer and develop a radical Christianity and a non-religious hermeneutic commensurate with tradition and modern life. The Bible, the church and the Kingdom of God can and must have an effect today upon a hurting world.

May we take the mandate of Christ to "Occupy: Take Territory!" until He comes.

Chapter V

The Kingdom And The Incarnation

"Be such a man, and live such a life, that if every man were such as you, and every life a life like yours, this earth would be God's paradise."

— Phillips Brooks

Chapter V

THE KINGDOM AND THE INCARNATION

In order to maintain a Biblical perspective, every system of doctrine must have an orthodox view of Christology. This orthodoxy must include the Incarnation, the death of Jesus Christ as a sacrifice for sin and a redemption of all that was lost, and a firm belief in the bodily resurrection and ascension of Jesus Christ. Furthermore, if we are to develop an adequate theology of the Kingdom, it must be firmly rooted in our Christology and in the centrality of the cross.

The Last Days

First of all, let us consider the word "eschatology." Eschatology is not a particular theory regarding the outcome of history. It is rather the study of every phase of the end of the world, as revealed in Jesus Christ. The word eschatology stems from the Greek word "eschaton," which is translated "last." Traditionally defined, eschatology is the doctrine of last things.

These last days begin with the inauguration of the Kingdom at Jesus' birth, and end with the consummation of the Kingdom at His second coming. The word "eschaton" occurs 50 times in the New Testament.

Eschatology is usually understood to concern the future. However, that is not the meaning of eschatology as used in Scripture. It is a definite period of time. It could, however, be a lengthy period of time or a limited period of time. Hebrews 1 states, "Christ was manifested and revealed in the eschaton—or these 'last days'." I Peter 1:20 states that it was for our benefit that Jesus was revealed in the eschaton—or these "last days." The eschaton in these verses is defined as a period already present when Jesus walked the earth. Therefore, we must assume that the eschaton began with the manifestation, or literal presence, of Jesus Christ upon the earth.

We can also define the eschaton as this current age. The current age is defined as the age that began when Jesus was born, and terminates at His Second Coming. We can also assume from Scripture that this current age is the one that terminates all the ages of history.

The second question posed concerning the eschaton and embracing the entire history of the universe is "What is God's purpose in history?" The answer to that would simply be this, "Victory through our Lord Jesus Christ!"

I John 3:8 states, "For this purpose the Son of Man was manifested, that He might destroy the works of the devil." His very presence upon the earth was the beginning of the total destruction of the kingdom of Satan. His total purpose was the complete destruction of Satan's kingdom.

The Victory of the Incarnation

The question now raised is, "Has this Victory been completed?" The total victory has already been won by Jesus Christ upon the cross of Calvary. The foundation of this historic victory is not to be found in the future, when He comes again, but is rooted in something which has transpired in the past. That victory was won by Jesus Christ and was accomplished by His first coming. His second coming is only the consummation of the first. One prominent author has stated, "We are to preach His first coming and refer to His second." We should let His first coming literally grip our hearts. For in His first coming, God became Incarnate, the God who made the universe and upholds all things, came to the earth nestled in the womb of Mary. God was born a human being and became one of us.

The Incarnation is the magnificent invasion of God into history through our Lord Jesus Christ. Anything that will happen in the future, including His second coming, absolutely is secondary in majesty beside His first coming in the Incarnation. John 1:14 states, "We beheld His glory, the glory of the only begotten of the Father, full of grace and truth."

Now the question arises, "What did God Incarnate accomplish when He came the first time?" This question is answered in three phases.

First, He tasted death for every man (I Corinthians 15:3-4). He died for our sins. Christian orthodoxy is absolutely based on the substitutionary death of Jesus Christ for the sins of mankind.

Secondly, the Scripture proclaims that Jesus defeated Satan when Jesus came the first time. John 16:11 states, "The prince of this world is judged." The implication of this verse indicates that there was a totality in the victory of Jesus Christ over the kingdom of darkness. He took captivity captive. He wrestled the keys of death and of Hell from Satan. Therefore, it is only reasonable to deduct that there was a defeat of Satan through and by the cross. That defeat was not future, but historic.

Thirdly, referring to John 16:11 once again, the prince of this world was judged by God Incarnate. In other words, Jesus judged the world system. It is not a future judgment, but rather a historic judgment. The Babylonian world system will not be judged by God in the future in the same dimension in which it has already been judged. God has already pronounced judgment upon the Babylonian world system. It is a cursed city. It is a doomed metropolis. It is still attempting to function apart from God, but it has been judged by Jesus Christ upon the cross. The redemptive miracle emerging from the old world system is another city whose Builder and Master Architect is God. A City that is eternal in nature. A Kingdom unlike any other Kingdom that has gone before. A Kingdom that shall never fall.

Fourthly, Jesus became Lord of all upon the cross. He became Lord of the Church. No Church scholar would deny that He is Lord of the Church. He has been crowned Lord of all nations. He will not *become* Lord of all nations. He *is* Lord of all nations, now, in the real dimension. He is Lord of the Communist nations, now. He is Lord of the Third World. Even though many parts of the world rebel against Him, He sits on the Right Hand of the Father as the Lord of the entire world.

Because He is Lord, He has commissioned us to be His representatives to take His rule to all of the nations of the world over which He has already become Lord as the result of His first coming.

Fifthly, He has created a new race. The Scripture indicates that He created a new species. These are not just reformed human beings. These are not just a people who stuck to a New Year's Resolution. They are not just patched up for a period of time. But He has created a new race of people. He has created a new Kingdom of people, a people in whom He dwells. All of these things are not to be accomplished when He comes again, but they are already accomplished facts. He has tasted death for every man. He has defeated Satan. He has judged the world. He has *already* become Lord of all. He has already created a new race of people.

Most wonderful of all, perhaps, is the fact that a new victorious reign of Jesus Christ has already been established. I Corinthians 15:25 states, "He shall reign until all things be placed under His feet." This verse would indicate that the reign of Christ is not something that shall be just during the Millennium. But even during this time, when there is rebellion evident upon this planet, there is already a reign of Jesus Christ. How wonderful are those words to our ears! We can build our hope not on a future victory, but on a past victory. The victory of Jesus Christ is something which has officially taken place.

The purpose of the teaching of the Kingdom of God is not only to preach that the Kingdom is something to be anticipated, although its full establishment will be future; the preaching of the Kingdom centers on how we are to be representatives of a Kingdom that already exists. It exists first of all in history. Satan has been judged and the Kingdom of God has been established. Secondly, it exists in our hearts. Thirdly, His rule and reign are to be brought to dynamic demonstration upon the society and the problems of our day. Jesus proclaimed to his disciples that the Kingdom was at hand. He commanded them to go out and take authority over sickness and disease and even death itself. They were to enforce His rule and reign, which now existed.

Satan is manifested in a myriad of ways. We recognize prejudice, hunger, poverty, crime, war, hatred, murder, lack of commitment, sickness and greed as works of the devil. In these ways Satan's kingdom is manifested. But, we have been transferred from the kingdom of darkness to the Kingdom of God's dear Son, and have been given authority over the kingdom of darkness, as it is manifested in all of these areas.

The eschaton is not something that has just recently occurred. The last days refer to the establishment of the Kingdom of God upon this planet. The eschaton is that time period which begins with the revelation of Jesus Christ on the earth, through the Incarnation, and ends with the consummation of the Kingdom at His second coming.

The Kingdom is future, as it will not be fully established until Jesus physically returns. The Kingdom is also present. It is a Kingdom that now exists. The centrality of the Kingdom of God is founded not on something that Christ will do in the future. It is founded upon a work and a ministry that was established many years ago at the cross. Jesus paid the price to redeem back from Satan all that was lost through the rebellion that took place even before the earth was in its present form.

Chapter VI

The Kingdom And The Universe

"What a rich gain for poor Colossae, that they, being in Him, were in it!"

— H.C.G. Maule

Chapter VI

THE KINGDOM AND THE UNIVERSE

The entire purpose of God is to fully enthrone His Son, the Lord Jesus Christ, as the Sovereign of the entire universe. All of Christian theology revolves around that central purpose: the reign of Jesus Christ. That central purpose is to enthrone Jesus Christ over the entire universal creation, so that He may return the Kingdom to the Father (I Corinthians 15:24). Therefore, the entire Scripture must be a handbook of how Jesus Christ is to be enthroned. It is essential that we develop a theology of the Kingdom of God, or the reign of Christ, from the entire context of the Scripture.

There are two central chapters that build the foundation for the theology of the Kingdom. The first is Genesis 1 and the second is Colossians 1. The first chapter of Colossians may be the greatest Kingdom chapter in the Bible.

The central theme of a Kingdom theology is birthed in Colossians 1:13. This verse states, "He has delivered us from the power of darkness (the kingdom of darkness) and translated us into the Kingdom of the Son of His love." God has provided in the process of new birth a transference of human beings from the reign of darkness into the reign of His beloved Son. Salvation has literally caused me to be transformed into a new person and has made me a citizen of another totally different Kingdom. This Kingdom is not something that *will* transpire, but rather something that comprises my present day existence. I now live in that new Kingdom.

Judeo-Christian Belief
vs.
Greek Philosophy

We can now understand how diametrically opposed the Judeo-Christian belief is to the belief system of the world. A Judeo-Christian ethic resists the tenets of Greek philosophy which was born from the kingdom of darkness. The introductory conflict in this chapter between the Greek view and the Kingdom view is the material universe.

The Greek Gnostics believed that the material universe was evil and that all matter was evil; the contradictory view of the Kingdom of God was that all things were created by and for Jesus Christ (Colossians 1:16). This would indicate that the entire material universe is a spiritual entity created by Jesus Christ and for Jesus Christ. Therefore, it is a Kingdom over which He has rulership or dominion.

During the 1940's I remember a pamphlet being circulated called "The God of the Atom" which described the author's perusal of Biblical truth in the atomic structure of the universe. He related his interviews with scores of atomic scientists who were involved in the development of the atomic bomb. Each scientist described the negative and positive factors of the atom, but none of these scientists found a word adequate to describe the nucleus of the atom. Most of the scientists, groping for a word, said the only way to describe the nucleus of the atom is to call it "spirit." This concurs with Colossians 1:17 which states, "...and is before all things, and in Him all things consist," or, in other words, "all things are held together." This would indicate that the material universe, the atomic structure of the universe, the molecular structure of the universe, is held together not by something that is material, but rather by something that is spirit. That "Spirit" is the reign of Jesus Christ. The entire molecular structure of the universe was created by Christ and is held together by His dominion. This clarifies how absolutely contradictory Greek thought is to Christian thought. The Greek philosophers observed that material things were evil, whereas Christians, under the tutorship of the great Apostle Paul, now learn that the material universe is actually spiritual, and that all material substance is under the rule or reign of Jesus Christ.

It is interesting how different philosophically the Christian view of material things is than the Greek view. The world would assume that material things are evil or non-spiritual. Therefore, the world system infers that the abundance of material possessions would be evil and would turn us away from God. The Apostle indicates in this chapter that material things are, in reality, spiritual and have as their center the Spirit of Jesus Christ. When speaking of money, Jesus said that if we seek the Kingdom of God, all of these things would be added unto us (Matthew 6:33). "It is the Father's good pleasure to give you the Kingdom," were the words of Jesus in Luke 12:32. This indicates that the Kingdom consists, at least in part, of material things, and that when God gives us things, He is in actuality giving us the Kingdom. The ultimate theological conclusion of this approach would be that the material universe was created by God, and that all material things exist in His Kingdom and are ruled over by His authority.

The Church and the Kingdom

As a pastor, I have often rhetorically preceded an offering with the phrase, "We are taking this offering for the expansion of the Kingdom of God." This is not necessarily an erroneous statement. Each time the church expands, the Kingdom expands. However, my rhetorical phrase is an incomplete statement. I had always believed that the Kingdom of God was to be equated with the church. I believed that the church was the Kingdom and the Kingdom was the church. When a person came to Christ, my belief was that he came into the church and, therefore, into the Kingdom.

As I began to realize that all of the created universe was the Kingdom of God, I began to understand the difference between the church and the Kingdom. The Kingdom was *everything* that God had made, embracing the visible and the invisible. All of this is the Kingdom of God. The church, conversely, is the "house within a house," the delegated people of God in which the presence of God dwells. The church is a chosen people who are to be the witnesses of the Kingdom of God and the reign of Christ in the world.

The Visible and the Invisible

This chapter also presents the Kingdom as not only the visible universe, but also as the invisible. Colossians 1:16 states that the invisible is defined as thrones, dominions, principalities and powers, or a governmental system through which Jesus Christ rules the material universe. This statement is a vital link in the understanding of Kingdom theology. The kingdom is the entire visible universe over which Jesus Christ reigns, as indicated in verse 17. The Kingdom is also the invisible. The invisible can be defined as the governmental system through which and by which Jesus Christ rules the visible or material universe.

It was into this visible universe ruled by Jesus Christ through a governmental system of thrones, dominions, principalities and powers that a rebellion came, engineered by an archangel named Lucifer.

Lucifer and the Kingdom

In light of the rulership of Jesus Christ over the visible universe, I have made a supposition which I present as only a possibility in helping to understand Kingdom theology. Perhaps it is possible that there were three thrones in the universe. (You will note that verse 16 does use the plural, "thrones.") It is possible that on these three thrones sat the three archangels: Michael, Gabriel and Lucifer. It is also possible that these three archangels reigned over the entire material universe, which was possibly divided into three dominions. A third of the visible universe was under Lucifer, a third under Michael and a third under Gabriel. Among the verses of the Bible which refer to the rebellions of Lucifer, the Scripture states that a third of the stars fell (Revelation 12:4), and another verse states that a third of the angels fell (Revelations 12:9). Is it possible that what the verses in actuality say is that the one-third of the angels over which Lucifer reigned fell captive to his authority and rebellion, and that a third of the stars, or visible creation which was under the control of Lucifer, fell with him? After the rebellion, Lucifer was the rebel leader over one-third of the material universe. This view is further enhanced by the fact that the Bible says that he was cast down to the earth where he set up the gates of hell. The gates of hell simply means the capital city of hell or the government of hell. This is the position of Satan in Scripture. Perhaps he rules over one-third of the rebel universe from his capital city, the planet Earth.

This treatise is further supported by Colossians 1:20 which states, "...and by Him to reconcile all things to Himself, by Him whether they are things on earth or things in heaven." This verse would indicate that there is coming a day when the visible universe will be reconciled to Christ by Christ and through the Blood of the Cross. When the capital city falls to the authority of Jesus Christ again, it seems that the whole universe will be reconciled.

Man and the Kingdom

God began the process of reconciliation in the first chapter of Genesis as He began to bring light out of darkness, order out of chaos, and form out of void. God began the process of re-creation in the capital city of darkness: the earth. God brought light, form, order and life to the earth. He carves out, in the midst of the rebel city, a beautiful Utopia called the Garden of Eden. In the Garden of Eden, He places His masterpiece of creation, Adam. The Bible states that man is God's image, God's likeness, the offspring of God and like God. He is filled with God's life and he thinks God's thoughts and does God's will.

The Book of Genesis explosively details man's divine destiny and purpose. That purpose in the Book of Genesis is to tend God's garden and to subdue God's earth which is still inhabited by Satan. This would indicate that man was the agent of God to reclaim the earth for the dominion of the rightful ruler of the universe. It is possible that if man had fulfilled that Divine prerogative, Satan would have been overthrown and the capital city of earth would have fallen to God's delegated authority. If this had been completed, the entire universe would have been reconciled.

Satan's presence is soon felt by this man. Satan invaded the perfection of the Garden to tempt the man who was made in God's image. His very presence in the Garden indicates his abode on the earth. The earth was not subdued from the sinister forces of evil by God's first act of re-creation. Perhaps the re-creation in Genesis 1 was only the first step in the magnificent plan of God to rule again over every part of His rebellious universal kingdom. God did not attempt to accomplish this purpose by Himself, but rather made for Himself a man. God duly commissioned man with His full authority and power to reclaim the rebel capital city—Earth—from Satan.

In light of these thoughts, the Bible takes on a whole new Kingdom significance. The Kingdom of God *is* the entire universe. Into that universe came a rebellion led by Satan. Satan was cast out to make his capital city on Planet Earth. Man was then created with the specific purpose to bring that planet back under the control of God, as God's delegated authority and agent.

The Arrival of the King and His Kingdom

When man rebelled, he was virtually overcome by the rebellion itself. Into this rebel planet, with its rebel people, came Jesus Christ, the only begotten Son of God. His announcement, upon arrival, was, "The Kingdom of God is at hand!" The King of the universe was present on Planet Earth, and when He is present, His Kingdom is present with Him.

Jesus gathered around Him twelve intimate followers. They argued over when He would set up a physical kingdom. They were thinking of a more insignificant kingdom than was His plan. Their thoughts were to control the Jewish nation, to set up a gold chair in Jerusalem and to rule the world from the City of Jerusalem. Jesus, according to Colossians 1, was planning a different Kingdom, even greater. Jesus was thinking of a Kingdom which would include the entire universe. His followers continued to argue over this and He reiterates that this is not their worry. Their concern should be whether they are filled with the presence of God's Holy Spirit.

The importance of this issue is illustrated in the fact that if the King of the universe is present on the planet, then the Kingdom of God is also present. When the Holy Spirit, Who is the Spirit of Christ, is dwelling in His believers, then the King is still present upon the planet. The church, then, is the expression of the Kingdom of God upon the planet.

The calling of the men in whom Christ dwells is to be the expression of Christ upon the planet; the purpose of the church in whom Christ dwells is the same. Christ calls them to Himself and exhorts them to preach the Kingdom of God. He tells them to heal the sick, cleanse the leper and to raise the dead. He reminds them, "Freely you have received, freely give" (Matthew 10:8). The Son of God reveals areas in which Satan rules on this planet and how they, as His dwelling place, can take authority over Satan's domain.

The Hope of Glory

The twenty-seventh verse of the first chapter of Colossians is perhaps the most magnificent verse in this entire Scripture: "To whom God would make known what is the riches of the glory of this mystery among the Gentiles, which is Christ in you, the hope of glory!"

The "hope of glory," defined, is to bring all things under the Lordship of Christ. Wherein does that hope lie? Personally, it has always been placed upon the physical return of Christ to the planet. I had been like the disciples. They believed that upon His return there would be, in the coming Kingdom, a Utopia. But Paul, who understood delegated authority, clearly believes that heaven's hope is not only in the physical return of Christ, but also in the people in whom He dwells. His people are to be the subduers: the ones who take dominion in this earth over the kingdom of Satan.

As previously stated, this theology can be developed to a greater extent than Christ originally intended it to be. He warned the disciples not to consider themselves the people who would "take over" the world. They would always experience persecution. The wheat and tares would continuously grow together. The people of God were to be salt, light and leaven in every situation and circumstance.

The inference in Scripture is that the full "take over" of the planet will not occur until Jesus physically returns and joins His church once again. That truth does not preclude the very purpose of the church. That purpose is to enforce the victory Jesus Christ has already won on the Cross.

Colossians 1 concludes the matter. Not only will all things on earth be reconciled by Him, but also all things will be reconciled in heaven. The simple meaning of this final piece of Kingdom theology is that one day, when this planet finally falls to the reign of Christ, He will return to the planet with His church who have gone to meet Him in the air. Then, in a triumphant finale, all things on this planet will be reconciled and returned to the Rightful Ruler of the universe. The significant twentieth verse indicates that when the capital city falls, things in heaven will also be reconciled. The third of the universe taken captive by Lucifer will be returned to the reign of Christ. Once again, all visible things in heaven will be ruled by the invisible Kingdom of Jesus Christ. The thrones, dominions, principalities and powers which He has established will fall in submission to His Rulership.

At this point, the caution is that the Scripture *nowhere* indicates the reconciliation of everything that has rebelled. The Scripture is very clear that Satan and his rebel angels will be cast away forever. The reconciliation of Colossians 1:20 does not imply that Satan and his angels will be converted. The people on earth who fail to come under the Lordship of Christ neither will be reconciled. Their own willful choice has elected that they will remain in the rebel kingdom. Therefore, they will be cast into outer darkness forever, where there will be wailing and gnashing of teeth.

In spite of the irreconciliation in the aforementioned areas, the ultimate victory of the Cross will be established. He has made peace through the blood of the Cross (verse 20b). Through the price that He paid on the Cross, Jesus Christ has, once again, become Ruler of the universe. The church is the enforcer of His victory. Each time we pray for the sick and healing is accomplished, we enforce His victory. When we go to work and demonstrate the laws of the Kingdom in our business, we enforce His reign upon the earth. When we live a life of holiness and do not lie, cheat or steal, we enforce His victory on this planet. Our lives are to be Kingdom lives. We are a people who live under the reign of Christ and, therefore, witness to the world the true Kingdom of Christ on this planet.

Chapter VII

The Kingdom And The Earth

"Every thought which genius and piety throw into the world alters the world.

— Emerson

Chapter VII

THE KINGDOM AND THE EARTH

In an intense study of Kingdom theology, it must be noted that the earth plays an important role in the plan of God. Previously, earth has been defined as "the gates of hell" or the capital city of hell. Lucifer has ruled over his portion of the universe from this planet for thousands of years. God provided a re-creation for this planet. He placed a magnificent garden upon earth which was a Utopia of His rule and reign. He sent His only begotten Son to this very planet.

This indicates that the planet called "Earth" has great significance in the plan of God. Many have developed the theology of the planet from a single verse of Scripture in the Book of Peter which talks about the planet being cleansed by fire (I Peter 1:7). Fire is a cleansing process. The Scripture indicates that there will be a new heaven and new earth. Those words do not necessarily indicate that the old will totally disappear. They do indicate, however, that the earth shall be remade under the rulership and reign of Jesus Christ.

We must then develop an adequate theology of the Divine plan that this planet occupies. First of all, it is imperative to realize that the planet earth is the center of universal redemption through the Cross, according to Colossians 1. The glorious twentieth verse indicates that whatever happens in the universe will happen because of the blood of the Cross. Whatever is beyond our planetary system has been universally redeemed through one single Cross. The earth was the center of that redemption and will universally remain the center of redemption.

Theology of the Earth

Jesus stated in the Sermon on the Mount, "The meek shall inherit the earth." Often in Christianity we become so "heavenly-minded" that Jesus' emphasis on the inheritance of the earth is de-emphasized. Why did Jesus assert that the meek would inherit the earth, and not heaven? There is a possibility that His emphasis was more on an earthly reward for the righteous, rather than a heavenly reward.

God made a covenant with Abraham and promised to bequeath him a land. Many theologians believe that this bequest was the land of Palestine. Abraham finally arrived in the land of Palestine and lived there with his family for many years. He inherited the land and began to develop this beautiful parcel of ground as the home of his family. It was the fulfillment of a promise that God made to him when he first encountered the covenant. However, this is not the end of the Abrahamic covenant. The Book of Romans states that the land which Abraham inherited was not only a small parcel of ground known as Palestine, but that "Abraham was the heir of the world" (Romans 4:13). Again, God is emphasizing His covenant with the earth. God will give the earth to the seed of Abraham. The seed of Abraham is defined in the Book of Galatians as all who are in Christ (Galatians 3:7). This would re-emphasize the theology of Christ that the meek, or those who come under the reign of Christ, will inherit the earth.

Scripture consistently identifies God as having full ownership of the earth. Psalm 24:1 states, "The earth is the Lord's and the fullness thereof." At times, Christian theologians are prone to emphasize the principalities of the air, or the enemy Satan, as being "alive and well on Planet Earth." Nowhere in Scripture does the Bible state that Satan is the owner of the earth. He was cast down to the earth, and now attempts to rule the earth as the rebel leader. He has set up his capital city here, but he is nowhere defined in Scripture as having ownership of this planet. God has retained ownership of the planet. There will be a way, through which, and by which, Jesus Christ will again be total ruler of this planet and of this universe. This is accomplished through the purchase price paid by His death on the Cross.

The Bible also links the subject of repentance to the land. II Chronicles 7:14 states, "If My people, which are called by My name, shall humble themselves...and repent...then will I...heal their land." Repentance, culminating in revival, has as its ultimate result the healing of the land.

In the New Testament, when the Holy Spirit exhorted Christians to "come out of the world," He was not referring to physically leaving the planet. Rather, the Holy Spirit was making reference to coming out of the world *system*. In John 17:15 Jesus prayed, "I do not ask Thee to take them out of the world." It is the world system, or the Babylonian system, from which we are to come out. The world is the creation of God and it is owned by God. Orthodox Christian theology demands a deep reverence for the earth.

The very doctrine of Christ the Creator is in direct contrast to the Gnostics who have unsuccessfully attempted to separate God from material creation by calling material things "evil." As previously stated, Paul faced the heretical mind patterns of the Gnostics that attempted to separate Christ from creation by the resounding affirmation, "In Him all things were created in heaven and earth, visible and invisible" (Colossians 1:16). As Robert Webber states in "The Secular Saint," "For this reason the church has always affirmed the goodness of creation. The world, the cosmos, is to be affirmed. The created order is not profane."[19] If this is true, then it is important for the church to recognize the various mandates implied.

The Earthly Mandates

First of all, there is an ecological mandate. Genesis 1:28 states, "...replenish the earth." This can be simply translated, "When you cut down a tree, replace it with another one." Ecology is, therefore, affirmed in Scripture as a Biblical—more, and spiritual—mandate to God's people.

However, the earth is more than a physical planet with ecological concerns. It is a house in which God has placed His very image to dwell. It is, therefore, a community with social structure. It is a place where every man has been called to be "his brother's keeper." The earth is a place where the people of God have been divinely appointed to be the "social reformers" of a sick sociological structure which has brought pain to the people of the planet. The ecological and sociological problems of the earth are, in reality, spiritual problems. There are no earthly solutions to many of these problems. The healing of the land is not the responsibility of humanistic social reformers, but rather the mandate to God's people who are empowered by the Holy Spirit.

The mandate is clear. God's people are not only to evangelize the world, but also to preach the Kingdom of God as an alternative life-system. This alternative life-system will present creative "Daniel" answers to the problems of our earth.

Author's Intent

It is not my purpose to develop a theology of the earth that all Christians should embrace. It is my privilege, however, to challenge the people of God to develop their own theology. The question that I am raising is, "What purpose does the earth have in the economy of God?" It is vitally important to realize the significance that God has placed on the earth by making it the center of His redemptive system. How important is the Scriptural ecological mandate which challenges those who pull up a tree to replace it with another one? How many times have men pulled up trees, as they did in the Sahara Desert of Africa, until great areas of a continent have been overtaken by the sands of the desert, because man has not fulfilled the ecological mandate?

The church is the moral conscience of the world and, therefore, must take absolute responsibility for every ecological and sociological problem of this planet. It is God's planet. God designed the church to enforce His Kingdom rule in this planet until He returns.

Chapter VIII

The Kingdom And Its Conflict With The World System

"When His Kingdom comes,
What a difference!
When things are on earth,
as they are in heaven!
When all has been settled,
and my heart is His throne,
Oh, What a difference!
What a great transformation!
When His Kingdom comes!"

— Donnie and Reba Rambo McGuire

Chapter VIII

THE KINGDOM
AND
ITS CONFLICT WITH THE WORLD SYSTEM

The famed E.V. Hill recently stated, "The world is no friend of grace." This statement holds great truth. The church is a faith community which finds itself outside of its own culture. We have been translated from the kingdom of darkness into the Kingdom of God's dear Son.

Jesus told His disciples that He had come not to bring peace, but had come to bring a sword. By this He meant that they would always be in conflict with the society around them. He further stated that they would always undergo persecution. The persecution that they were to experience would indicate the alien society in which they existed. Theirs would be an upside-down Kingdom. They would be living in the midst of something that would be totally alien to who they were and what they were called to accomplish. We are a community that finds itself outside of its native culture.

One of the interesting points concerning a church in conflict is that we thrive in the midst of it. The early church was in conflict with the culture around it. The conflict became so intense in the City of Jerusalem that the church was scattered throughout the world. In spite of their dispersion, they found themselves again in conflict with the society around them. Each time they encountered conflict, it made the church become stronger. It is the Divine design of God that as a Body of Believers they would not only exist in the midst of conflict but that His Body would flourish under pressure.

Kingdom theology is the very essence of resolution of the conflict which exists between the church and the world. The world system of economics is opposite to God's system of economics. The world system of commerce is opposite to God's system of commerce. The world system of the arts is opposite to God's system of worship. Everything that the world offers is diametrically opposed to the things of the church of Christ.

History of Jewish Conflict

The Jewish faith certainly thrived best when under great persecution. Psalm 137 poses the question which the Jews asked as they were exiled into Babylonian captivity, "Can we sing songs in the midst of our captivity?'' Babylon had surrounded them, just as Babylonian society has pitched its tent around the church of Jesus Christ today. The question remains the same, ''Can we not only survive, but can we thrive triumphantly?''

The experience of the Jews in Babylonian captivity came to be a positive renewal experience. The exilic congregation learned to sing under pressure. In the Babylonian society, the synagogue was born. They had been extracted from temple worship and were not permitted to establish a new temple. As a result, their creativity birthed the synagogue. A synagogue was an extended family which could be formed by at least ten adult men. The synagogue did not need a priest, but the lay people could read the Scripture and study sacred writings. It was not a sacramental place, and, therefore, was not tied to the sacraments in the temple. Instead it was intrinsically bound to the Word of God itself.

It was in this exilic experience, under the pressure of Babylonian society, that the Old Testament largely came into existence. It was here that the Jewish people put together the Torah in the form that we know it today. God did not abandon them when they were under the pressure of Babylonian society, but He gave them Ezekiel the prophet. It was to this exiled people that Isaiah 40-55 was addressed, ''Comfort ye, comfort ye my people.''

Several other significant developments took place in the exilic existence. For the first time, the people of God went from an agricultural society to becoming an urban people. In this urban situation they developed a sense of mission. Prior to the Babylonian captivity, the Jews had always gone to Mt. Zion, God's dwelling place. Mt. Zion was no longer accessible, and as a result, their mission had dramatically changed. They would no longer go to Mt. Zion, but they would be sent to the world. The Jews perceived Babylon as a spiritual desert but Babylon had become to them a creative place where the new was born. It was here that Judaism not only created the synagogue and what we know as Old Testament Scriptures, but also where Judaism probably thrived in its greatest religious fervor ever.

The exilic Jews developed several different mindsets. The first mindset was that the past could happen again. There were those who dreamed of going back to Jerusalem and then found nothing but problems. Jerusalem was ruled by one tyrant after another until finally Antiochus Epiphanes marched into the city and sacrificed a pig on the altar of God.

There was a second group of people that were like fatalists. They simply said to themselves in their apocalyptic literature, ''Whatever will be, will be.'' They believed that God would just work it all out regardless of their response.

There was a glorious third alternative to the other pitiful mindsets. They knew that in their lifetime they would never go back to the City of Jerusalem. They knew that in their lifetime they would never be able to re-establish the Davidic Kingdom. But, they also knew that they would live life successfully, as Jews in dispersion had done in other nations. It was to this group, that had decided to live sacrifically as God's chosen people in dispersion, that the New Testament faith of Christianity ultimately came.

The second chapter of Acts accounts historically that it was these faithful dispersed Jews who came to the City of Jerusalem. These who made their pilgrimage to Jerusalem to worship were the Jews who were there at the time of the outpouring of Pentecost. They were a people who would not relive the past. They were a people who emphatically said, "We will not fill the apocalyptic vision of going into oblivion and seeing God judge us. But we are a people who will live successfully as God's people, even under the pressure of dispersion." It was under that dispersion that God found them and that the New Testament message of Jesus Christ as Messiah came. It was upon these people who had lived with perseverance under the pressure cooker of Babylonian civilization that Jesus came to pour out His Spirit (Acts 2).

It is interesting to note how these dispersed people lived. They formed communities in their homes, simply telling the great Bible stories. These Bible stories included the great story of Daniel and the story of how God had met the exiled Jews in the land of Babylon. These historic accounts chronicled the ascending of the dispersed Jews to high responsible positions in civil service. Many like Daniel and the three Hebrew children penetrated the culture of a foreign society and became active members in a world that was hostile to them.

The Kingdom in Triumph

While I was attending a recent retreat in Maui, Dr. Harold Englund asked the names of the three Hebrew children. Almost every one of the Bible scholars around the table said, "Shadrach, Meshach and Abednego." The moderator of the session corrected, "That was not their names. Their names were Hanaiah, Mishael and Azariah." Though even the Bible calls them by their Babylonian names, they had Hebrew identities as expressed through their Hebrew names. The name of Abednego was Azariah, which means "the Lord hath helped us." If we allow it to, the Babylonian culture will rename our children. Let us remember that we are aliens always in conflict with the world around us.

If we can recognize the conflicts that we will always be exposed to in our society, we can live successfully in the midst of a hostile environment. As we recognize the conflict, we must also recognize our calling. Jesus said we would be salt, light and leaven to a dying, dark world. We must grow as wheat, along with the tares. This is our identity.

The major news to this peculiar people who have been called out of the kingdom of darkness is that no matter what happens, God will be with us! (John 16:32,33; Hebrews 13:5) We must never forget that we live in a hostile environment. As E.V. Hill said, "The world is no friend of grace." The world around us doesn't know how to take us, nor how to understand us, for we are in constant conflict with the world. If we recognize our conflict, we can also recognize that we are on the side of the Victor. There is coming a day when the final conflict will be won and we will take the Kingdom in triumph!

Chapter IX

The Kingdom And Worship

"For we wrestle not against flesh and blood, but against principalities and powers, against the spirit of wickedness in high places."

— Paul the Apostle
In his letter to the Ephesians

Chapter IX

THE KINGDOM AND WORSHIP

As the Christian begins to recognize a responsibility to the alien society around him, he begins to develop methodologies of trying to enforce the reign of Christ in the world. Some attempt to enforce His reign by picketing abortion clinics, by running for government office, by infiltrating the fabric of a company with Christians, or, in essence, by resorting to enforcing our belief system on the world. I do not necessarily decry any of these means or methods. However, I do not believe that they are at the very crux of the matter.

The Apostle Paul said that we wrestle not against flesh and blood but against principalities and powers (Ephesians 6:12). Our Kingdom fight is not one that can be won by politicians. Our Kingdom fight cannot be totally won by earthly means. Our battle can only be won in spiritual realms; the Kingdom battle is a spiritual battle.

The Enthroning of Christ

I believe the new emphasis on worship in the church is going to assist in enforcing the reign of Christ in the world as never before.

I was recently in Manila, Philippines, during a time of great civil unrest and conflict. The country was undergoing an attempted coup on the government. We were stopped often by armed guards in the streets and searched for weapons. We were searched as we would go in and out of our hotel. The whole country was in conflict.

I was in the Philippines because I had been invited to preach in a large church there. As I sat on that platform and watched the congregation with their hands lifted in glorious worship, I began to see, in the Spirit, something magnificent happening. I saw all of the conflict that was existing around the church. I saw the forces of evil that were rising up against peace in the nation around us. I saw the conflicts in the economic world and the huge amount of money that had been extracted from the nation, and the people suffering under the tremendous bondage of poverty. I saw that God had an answer for all of the dilemmas of the nation. But, I wondered, how would God's answer be delivered?

Would a new government, dedicated to justice and righteousness, arise? Was it possible that it would be accomplished through the election of a born-again president? Would there be a congress elected in the future which would establish a new constitution based upon a Christian foundation? How would peace, tranquility and prosperity come back to this nation? It was then that God showed me that the battle was in the heavenlies. I saw that there were forces of darkness that were trying to keep the country in poverty. There were forces that were trying to keep the country in conflict. There were dark forces that were trying to keep the country from being blessed. But, the battle was not at Malacanang Palace. The battle was not in the soon-to-be-elected Congress. The battle, in reality, was in the heavenlies. It was a battle between the kingdom of darkness and the Kingdom of God.

And then, as I saw the people in worship, and as I saw thousands of hands raised to the Lord, something inside of me said emphatically, "These people are crowning Jesus as King in their worship!" The Spirit continued to say, "As these people crown Jesus through worship, and as thousands of Filipinos join them in worship, My Kingdom and My peace can come to this nation. It will not happen politically. It will not happen by force. It will happen as the people which are called by My Name enthrone Me in worship."

There is a great truth in Revelation chapter 8 that has revolutionized my thinking about the establishment of the reign of Christ upon this Planet. Beginning with Revelation 8:3:

> "Then another angel having a golden censer, came up and stood at the altar. He was given much incense that he should offer it with the prayers of all the saints upon the golden altar which was before the throne. And the smoke of the incense, with the prayers of the saints, ascended before God from the angel's hand. Then the angel took the censer, filled it with fire from the altar and threw it to the earth, and there were noises, thunderings, lightnings, and an earthquake. So the seven angels who had seven trumpets prepared themselves to sound."

It is obvious that the sounding of these trumpets brought judgment to the evil society of the world. Judgment, however, was brought in a most interesting way upon the evil system.

First of all, there were the prayers of the saints. They had ascended to God over the ages. As I watched that Filipino congregation, I saw their prayers and worship ascend before God. God was saying to me as I read this chapter, "I am taking every voice that goes to me in worship, every voice that goes to me in prayer, and I am assembling that before the throne of God." I believe that every time we pray for our nation, every time we pray for our government officials and every time we pray for change to happen in our world, God takes those prayers and places them upon the golden altar.

The Scripture then says that He mixes the prayers of the saints with much incense. As I view these verses, it is my belief that God takes the prayers of the saints, commingles them with the coals from the altar of God, and then thrusts them back to the earth as reformation, judgment and change. As much as I believe that we are to be involved in the extension of the Kingdom of God upon the earth, I do not believe that our involvement should be political or economic involvement alone. The Kingdom of God will not merely come by fulfilling an ecological mandate, although that is necessary. The Kingdom of God will not be ultimately accomplished by running for office and becoming a righteous ruler in a nation of iniquity. The most important form of our involvement will be at the altar of God. God will take our prayers. God will take our worship. He will mix them together with the coals off of the altar and thrust it back at the earth as reformation, judgment and change.

As I continued to watch that great Filipino congregation lift their voices in praise and worship to God, I literally saw a vision of God taking those prayers and worship, mixing them with the coals from His altar, and thrusting it back at that nation as change. As I sat there on that platform, it seemed that if the Christians of that nation would recognize the power of their worship and the power of their prayers, God would sovereignly enforce His rule in a new dimension upon our planet.

The Kingdom battle is not with the forces of men, but it is with principalities and powers. It is with spiritual forces. This battle will be victoriously won in prayer and worship.

Chapter X

The Kingdom And Its People

"Let the admirable light of truth shining in them teach us that the mind of man, though fallen and perverted from its wholeness, is nevertheless clothed and ornamented with God's excellent gifts."

— John Calvin

Chapter X

THE KINGDOM AND ITS PEOPLE

Developing a Judeo-Christian Anthropology

Daniel, the exilic prophet in Babylon, had many amazing experiences. He and his three contemporaries stood against the Babylonian culture and endured unbelievable persecution twice. Daniel miraculously interpreted the king's dreams through the power of the Holy Spirit. He is one of the great mystics of all ages. He not only had the ability to see things in the spirit, but also the incredible ability to interpret, from the eyes of God, what others have seen by the revelation of the Holy Spirit. He is a mystic who stands head and shoulders above all others and a prophet extraordinaire.

Daniel meets with a great dilemma for the first time in his life in the Book of Daniel, chapter 7. The chapter ends with these words, "As for me, Daniel, my thoughts greatly troubled me, and my countenance changed in me; but I kept the matter in my heart" (verse 28). Though this great exilic prophet of God had previously known all of the great secrets which God desired to reveal to His people, this time Daniel is "greatly troubled" with what God has said to him. This is the first time that Daniel has ever received a revelation for himself. Though he was a prophet and had the ability to interpret the king's dreams, this is the first recorded dream of the prophet himself. Daniel's troubled state did not come from the fact that this was a dream that God had given him directly. The problem lay in the content of that dream. For God had repeatedly said to the prophet that "the saints of the most high shall receive the Kingdom" (verse 18). In verse 22 God repeats Himself, "...and the time came for the saints to possess the Kingdom." The very theme of this chapter is that the followers of God, known as saints, will be the people to whom the Kingdom will be given.

Daniel was well acquainted with Jewish thought. He recognized from the earliest writings of the Pentateuch that God had exhorted His people to "subdue the earth." It was God's plan that God's people would bring the rule of God to the entire earth. This was the very essence of Jewish philosophy and theology. Daniel also saw the Kingdom through the eyes of former prophets who believed it a monarchy rule to which all people would submit. The dream that God had given to Daniel was diametrically opposed to his perception of Jewish theology. This was what troubled Daniel.

Daniel knew that Israel desired to be like other nations and to have a king. Inside every human there is a secret but strong appeal to be "ruled over." It is this very desire that leads men into religious beliefs in which rules and regulations dominate the people. In these religious systems, people have no privilege of making moral or theological decisions for themselves. They give up their right to establish cultural behavior patterns within the confines of God's law. The religious system establishes the theology, the culture and behavior patterns for the people. The people are dominated by what the religious system thinks and believes. They have no mind of their own. It is this very desire to "have a king" that can lead men into religious systems of domination.

Conversely, the concept in the Old Testament was that the nation was to be a "kingdom of priests." The people were to represent God to the world and the world to God. The fact that every man was a priest unto God leads to the belief that God's intention for Israel was that every man was to be a leader himself. The New Testament consistently presented the concept to the church that we are a people who are "kings and priests unto God."

The dichotomy of this viewpoint greatly troubled the prophet. He knew the inbred nature of the human being. The human being wrestles against the premise that God has ordained him to lead. God wants man to be a decision maker.

The social fabric of human nature is inbuilt with the need for domination. We build religious institutions that do not teach men to think for themselves or to make decisions for themselves. These religious institutions foster a rulership and a domination by their decisions and teachings. The economic system again is a reflection of a culture that does not teach people to be decision makers, but rather to have their decisions made for them. The political systems of the world are to a great extent designed in the same manner. The very birthing of the democratic societies came out of the reformation. This was a new concept, that God desired the people to have the ability to rule themselves under the law of God.

The purpose of this chapter is to study people—who they are and for what purpose God created them. This chapter will identify the people to whom God will give His rule. In past chapters we have defined the role of man. The Genesis man was to export the culture that God had placed in the Garden of Eden to the four corners of the earth. He was to be the vehicle by which God would take dominion and subdue the earth. This chapter will look at the Biblical theology of the persons who are to be kings in this great Kingdom. The chapter will lay the foundation of the establishment of a Judeo-Christian anthropology for the church.

Influence of Gnosticism

A controversy rages in the church today concerning the definition of mankind theologically. The rise of the secular humanistic self-help movement is the result of the failure of the Christian church to properly define man, his role and his potential. Christians have developed a Greek view of man, rather than a Judeo-Christian anthropology. Our present view of the human being is the result of embracing the fatalistic view of the Greeks. Greek philosophy begins with Gnosticism and the philosophical view that all matter is evil. The Book of Colossians is the direct attack of the apostle Paul against Gnosticism. God, through Paul, declares that "all things were created for and by God" (Colossians 1:16). Paul's philosophy in the Book of Colossians establishes irrevocably that matter is the creation of God, that it is under the rule and reign of God, and is therefore an intrinsic part of God's Kingdom.

Out of Greek Gnosticism came Greek Asceticism. Greek Asceticism taught that because matter was evil, therefore, the outer man was evil. It would be necessary to punish the outer man and to deny him of pleasure or comfort in order to overcome evil. The inner spiritual man would then grow and become stronger than the outer evil man. This view was subversively brought into Christianity through the teachings of St. Thomas Aquinas. It has infiltrated the teachings of the church to this day. An example of the result of embracing these anti-Judeo Christian philosophical views was the establishment of the poverty vows within the church. The modern antagonism to the Christian participation in the prosperity covenant of Abraham is the result of the influence of Greek Gnosticism and Asceticism.

The Image of God

The Bible begins with a unique pronouncement that man was made in the "image of God." In the Book of Psalms, David asks the question, "What is man that thou art mindful of him? And the son of man, that thou visitest him?" (Psalms 8:4). God echoes from heaven the marvelous reiteration of His original pronouncement, "For thou hast made him a little lower than Elohim and crowned him with glory and honor, and given him dominion over the works of thy hands" (Psalms 8:5,6).

The very phrase "image of God" is profoundly interesting in establishing a Judeo-Christian anthropology of man. The original word in the Hebrew indicates that the person made in the image of God is an exact representation of God and is capable of doing God's work because he is *like God.* This statement presents great conflict with our present Christian anthropology. But, we cannot deny the original meaning of the word "image." It has been said that either we believe that man was made in the image of God or that he came from a monkey. Defining man as "God's offspring" is not only essential in developing a Christian anthropology, but if we do not recognize the meaning and full implications of this term, then we will find ourselves in the humanistic camp of agnostics and atheists who believe that we descended from monkeys.

Calvin's Influence

During the first part of the Reformation, Luther did not deal with the subject of Christian anthropology. Upon the emergence of the famed John Calvin, for the first time since the Canon was established, the church wrestled with a Judeo-Christian anthropology. One of the five points of Calvinism is usually described as "total depravity." This terminology came neither from Calvin nor from the later Canons of Dort (1619), but became a popular term in the later 17th and 18th century disputes with the Armenians.

The Westminster Confession of 1646 does not even use the term "total depravity." This term, however, could be considered the natural outgrowth of Calvin's viewpoint, since Calvin did believe in the absolute depravity of the spiritual nature of man.

Out of Calvinism came the belief in the "limited atonement." This theological viewpoint simply declares that because man is spiritually depraved he cannot initiate his own salvation. Therefore, salvation of man comes due to the choosing of God for an individual. It is God who initiates salvation, rather than man, according to limited atonement. Although Calvin believed that man was so depraved that he could not initiate his own salvation, it was Calvin who first began to theologically define the "characteristics" or "image of God" within the non-converted man.

I. John Hesselink, in his book, "On Being Reformed," states, "Many Calvinists have concluded that man is indeed worthless and capable of nothing good."[20] Unfortunately, very few people are aware of a crucial distinction which Calvin himself makes concerning fallen man. In the "Institutes,"[21] he distinguishes between man's knowledge and achievements in the realm of "heavenly things," in contrast to the realm of "earthly things." In the former realm, there is indeed nothing positive or good which the natural man can do. As far as spiritual things are concerned, even "the greatest geniuses are blinder than moles." Apart from the grace of God and the help of His spirit, "we are utterly blind and stupid in divine matters." In this, the vertical dimension, there is no question that man's depravity is indeed "total."

However, Dr. Hesselink also states in his book that "Calvin takes a much more positive view of man's capabilities and gifts on the horizontal level. In what we would call the secular realm (i.e., of 'earthly things'), even fallen man possesses a degree of conscience, common sense, natural instinct, reason, sense of justice and equity, as well as general ability in the realms of government, household management, mechanical skills, and the liberal arts. These natural gifts are corrupted through sin, but they are not to be denigrated. Thanks to God's 'general grace,' 'some sparks still gleam' in 'man's perverted and degenerate nature.' There is also in sinful man 'some sort of desire to search out the truth...'"[22]

It is interesting that Calvin also states, "Let that admirable light of truth shining in them teach us that the mind of man, though fallen and perverted from its wholeness, is nevertheless clothed and ornamented with God's excellent gifts."[23] As a result of Calvin's thinking, I. John Hesselink writes, "Man, for all his pervisity is not a wretched worm capable of only evil."[24]

It was Calvin who first began to define for the Christian church the difference between total depravity of man's spiritual nature and the residual image of God left in the human being after the fall and before his conversion.

The Dignity of Man

It was the very lack of this understanding that could create a holocaust from a people who were educated in the Christian community, but never taught the dignity of the human being or the image of God in those who were non-converted. Thus, you could have the ability to burn a heretic at the stake, or kill several million Jews who had failed to accept Jesus Christ, and feel that perhaps in these incidents you were doing God a favor. Therefore, we must re-examine our Christian anthropology and recognize that man is made in the image of God. Even in his preconversion state, man has dignity beyond our human ability to understand and the residual nature of God within himself. The ability to create, the ability to govern, the ability to develop beautiful works of art are all the residual nature of God within the human being, even in his preconversion state. An architectural masterpiece designed by a nonconverted person is not evil. It was inspired by the nature of God even in the non-converted architect.

Dietrich Bonhoeffer, in a German concentration camp during World War II, further developed a proper Judeo-Christian anthropology. Douglas C. Bowman, in an article entitled, "Bonhoeffer and the Possibility of Judaizing Christianity," states, "The trend of Bonhoeffer thinking might conclude that an appropriate outcome of the Bonhoeffer legacy would be the Judaizing of Christianity and involve theological adjustments concerning the notion of man, his nature, his possibilities and his capabilities."[25] He further states that Bonhoeffer's thinking would then result in a complete reversal of Augustinian development.

The failure to properly develop a Judeo-Christian anthropology has resulted in the rise of the self-help movement. Because Christians never studied the human being properly, it was left to men such as Sigmund Freud to define the human being. Men such as Napoleon Hill and other pantheists have defined the role and capabilities of the human being. Christian theology has been strangely silent and negligent in defining the human being for us.

While human intellectuals were grappling for their identity and while Christianity remained silent on defining the role and capabilities of the human being, the humanists were devising their own plan to define man. The writings of the pantheists present man as god and as the center of his own universe. Humanists symbolically have reenacted the entire scene of the building of the tower in Babylon. That is exactly what the tower of Babel represents: man becoming god and the center of his own universe. I applaud such men as Norman Vincent Peale and Robert Schuller who have attempted to define man from a Judeo-Christian viewpoint, building on the very premise of their Reformed forefather, John Calvin.

The Christian faith was born to a church who had strayed far from the very concepts that it espoused. While the church was attempting to judge a woman taken in adultery to the full extent of the law, Jesus defined her value to the world and to God. He reached out in compassion, restored her dignity and said, "Neither do I condemn thee, go and sin no more" (John 8:11). Jesus declared an emphatic demonstration of His own love, acceptance and forgiveness to the sinful woman. This was in direct contrast to the culture and tradition of the church of the day.

Christ demonstrates this again and again as He reaches out and touches the untouchable leper; as he calls the tax collector, Matthew, who has been excommunicated from the church, and invites him to become a disciple. Jesus does not overlook sin or faulty behavior, but He reaches out and returns dignity to the human being. Jesus gives purpose and recognizes that humans, though faulty in behavior, are not only the creation of God, but the creation made in the *very image* of God.

Chapter XI

The Kingdom And Its Servant Kings

"I can more easily see our Lord sweeping the streets of London than issuing edicts from its cathedral."

— Dick Sheppard

Chapter XI

THE KINGDOM AND ITS SERVANT KINGS

The Role of the Kingdom People

After defining the dignity of the human person, it is then imperative to discover his role upon the planet. It has already been noted that his role was to subdue the earth and to extend the culture of Eden to the entire world. This was the purpose of God's new Eden, the nation of Israel.

After Christ's birth, when he called his disciples, he empowered them with the power of the Kingdom. The disciples knew their role and were intent upon setting up the Kingdom upon the planet immediately. They had a vision of a gold chair with one of them sitting on either side. Jesus did not steal the hope of the Kingdom from them, but instead, told them that there would be interim steps in the establishment of the Kingdom. Of primary importance was the exhibiting of Kingdom behavior and then, as the Kingdom was extended throughout the planet, He would return to the planet and fully set up His Kingdom. The hope of His return was in no way intended to lessen their responsibility for the extension of the Kingdom on the planet.

As we define the role of the Kingdom people, it is of vital importance to identify the conversion experience and to differentiate between converted man and pre-converted man.

The conversion experience is an eternal moment in time when a human being is born again in the Spirit. His spirit is renewed in Christ and a whole New Person comes to dwell within him. The result of this experience is twofold. First, it readies him for heaven, and secondly, the personality of the Spirit abides within him. The Fruits of the Spirit and Gifts of the Spirit allow man to become even more creative than unregenerate man.

Pre-converted man is still magnificent because he was made in the image of God and the residual characteristics of God abide in him. However, in spite of all of his magnificence, pre-converted man is going to hell. He can be redeemed and it is God's will for him to be redeemed, if he chooses the conversion experience. When pre-converted man is redeemed he can fulfill God's role for himself on the planet.

Servant Kings

The question now raised is how this magnificent creature called man, redeemed by the blood of Christ, with the indwelling presence of God within him, is to fulfill his proper role upon the planet. Daniel looked across the years and heard God saying that He would give the Kingdom to His people. They would be a people who would be kings. How is it that we are to become kings?

The outstanding account of Jesus teaching kingship is recorded in the 13th chapter of the Gospel according to John. The chapter begins with the declaration that "His hour had come." Jesus was referring to a very important hour in His life, with these words. Jesus had gathered His disciples together for the Last Supper. At the end of the supper, He arose, laid aside his garments, took a towel and girded Himself (vs. 4). In the parallel passage in Luke 22, the disciples began to express the rivalry among themselves. They were arguing over who would be the greatest in the Kingdom. They were carrying their Kingdom theology to the extreme by suggesting that there should be a "great one" among them.

Jesus responds to the debate by explaining that this is the way the Gentile or world system works. He says that those who exercise authority or lordship benefit in many ways, including financial benefits from those who serve them. Jesus will not allow His Kingdom people to resort to this behavior. He then asks the question, "Which one is the greatest in this room, the one who sits at the table or the one who serves?" (Luke 22:27). Jesus shows by example that He is the one who has girded the towel upon Himself and served them.

What a marvelous way to define the governmental system of the Kingdom of God! Servanthood is the necessary prerequisite to greatness in God's Kingdom. God's servant rulers are those who initiate the process of servanthood. One of the problems with the world system today is that servants fail to lead, and those who do lead do not serve.

The philosophy of servant-leadership is the only system that will work in politics, business or the church. If a business will become a servant to its employees, its suppliers and its clients, it will succeed. If a business loses its servant identity and becomes greedy, its very existence will depend upon how many people serve the business. The result of greed in a business is immediate failure. There is only one system in all of God's universe that works. There is only one person qualified to lead, and that person is the servant.

The Servant Role of the Church

The greatest indictment that can be given to the church is that the church has become an institution that is served rather than one that serves. When people come into the church, we are prone to evaluate their strengths and mentally judge their ability to give financially to the church. We tend to see a qualified person join the church and rejoice that they can teach Sunday School, lead the choir or do something else productive within our body of believers. Our role in the world is not to require that people exist for the institution. God is building a Body of people that are designed to fulfill one role and that is to be a servant to the world.

The failure of the church to assume its servant role will result in discipling people who do not understand their servant role. In reality, what separates the church of Jesus Christ from Babylon is not only that they are a people prepared for heaven, but also a people who live an entirely separate lifestyle from the people of Babylon. In the Babylonian life system, those who strive to be in the leadership dimension are considered benefactors, or people who are served by others. In direct contrast, the leadership of the church are a people who are called to be servants. This Edenic culture is to be exported to society. The purpose of the covenant community is to make life better for the non-covenant community. The New Testament exhorts the church to disciple nations.

The church is attempting to do all kinds of things to straighten out our world today. We propose to elect political candidates and thereby "take over." We attempt to institute legal laws in order to change the status quo. The only role of change that Jesus taught His disciples was that they were to put on the towel and begin to serve others.

The life-style and teachings of John Calvin provide the church with a vivid illustration of the servant-leader role. John Calvin was able to blend a robust individual piety with a very practical concern for involvement in the world. Calvin saw the state as a divinely appointed agency. He viewed the church as a vehicle for establishing God's order in the world. He continually taught the Bible but also showed concern for such mundane matters as interest rates, sewers, safety in homes and immigration policies.

Calvin saw the church and its Body of related believers as the servant leader needed to bring comprehensive change to the world. There needs to be a blending of two views of our Christian faith. Like Calvin, we need to see Christ as the transformer of culture, with the church playing a role as the servant to the world. We need to follow the example of the Roman Catholic Church, as they build servant institutions such as schools, hospitals, etc.

We should stand behind men such as Oral Roberts in the building of medical institutions which will bring servant-leadership to the world of medicine. We need to exhibit servant-leadership to our inner-city ghettos and observe a miraculous transformation by the culture of the church of Jesus Christ. We need to see ourselves, both as individuals and as a corporate body, sent to bring healing to a hurting sociological structure.

Our concept of the purpose of the church needs a vital overhauling. The church is not to be served by the people who fill the pews. The main function of the church is to bring healing to a hurting people. As pastor of a church, my major role is to be a servant to my people. When my phone rings at one o'clock in the morning, I am to serve. When someone is having surgery at five o'clock in the morning and requests prayer at the hospital, I am to be a servant. If I lose sight of my servant role, I lose sight of the primary teachings of the Gospel.

The central message of the church is the message of salvation by grace. Christ died for our sins on the cross and has redeemed us from the curse of Satan. Standing alongside that message of redemption is the message that the redeemed are to become servant-leaders. It is the servant-leadership philosophy that separates the church from Babylon. We may think that it is our redeemed state which separates us, yet many unredeemed men are better servants than are redeemed men.

A born-again Christian who becomes a servant leader stands out from the society of Babylon and establishes the fact of his Christianity. The very experience of the baptism of the Holy Spirit in Acts 2 immediately caused the rich to become servants of the poor. The rich sold all that they had and divided their portions among the poor.

The church will only be able to change the world effectively when it finally embraces the centrality of the role of servanthood to Christian behavior.

Chapter XII

The Kingdom And Its Authority

"God warms his hands at man's heart when he prays."

— John Masefield

Chapter XII

THE KINGDOM AND ITS AUTHORITY

For many of us, prayer is a frustrating experience. Most of our prayers lack the authority that is outlined in the Scriptures. Jesus commanded sickness to leave and it left. Jesus commanded lepers to be cleansed and they were miraculously cleaned. Jesus commanded the dead to be raised and life was born again. Few contemporary Christians, if any, come near to possessing the authority that Jesus did in His prayer life.

Most Christians struggle with the dilemma of ineffective prayer. It is difficult to discern why we do not have authority over sin, sickness, disease and even Satan himself, as the Scriptures promised that we would.

While contemplating these theological questions, I began to search the Word of God concerning an answer to this personal dilemma. Many times I had commanded Satan to take his hands off sick bodies and yet they remained sick. I often had taken definitive authority over things in my own life, with no relief. As I began to study the Scriptures, I discovered that there was an authority structure in the Kingdom of God. The authority structure established by Jesus Himself is simply that unless a believer is under authority, he cannot obtain authority.

The Centurion's Secret

This great truth of the Kingdom is graphically illustrated in Scripture when the Centurion came to Christ. The Centurion recognized the secret to Jesus' ministry. He was able to recognize this important key because of its parallel in his own life. When the Centurion spoke, he spoke for Caesar and with the full authority of Caesar. If people did not obey his instructions, he could invoke the law of Caesar over their lives. The reason that the Centurion could speak for Caesar was that he was obedient to Caesar. As the Centurion addressed Christ, he pointed out their similarities. When the Centurion spoke, Caesar spoke, and when Jesus spoke, God spoke. Therefore, the Centurion told Christ, "If you will only speak the word, my servant will be healed" (Matthew 8:8). The secret that this Centurion understood has been revealed to very few of us. The secret is that when you are under someone's authority, you have their authority. Because Christ consistently obeyed the God of heaven and earth, He could speak for that same God.

The reason that most Christians do not receive answers to prayer is simple. If a believer does not fully submit himself to the rule and reign of Christ, their prayers will lack His authority.

The Reign of Christ

Many Christians do not know *how* to submit themselves to the reign of Christ and to the authority of God. Christian young people are brought up to believe that submitting themselves to Christ deals primarily with obeying the rules and regulations of the church. The church teaches its young people, in error, that if they do not smoke, drink, play cards or go to the movies, they are then fully obeying the rule and reign of Christ. To relegate the reign of Christ to a set of man-made rules is denying the deity of His rulership. There is more to the reign of Christ than adhering to a list of rules set forth by people in the church.

There is an authority structure to the Kingdom of God. If a believer would fully come under this authority structure and obey all of God's delegated authority, then that believer could experience ultimately the demonstration of His authority.

The delegated authority of God is not just some nebulous set of doctrines defined abstractly according to denomination, geographical location or historical setting. There is an absolute structure set forth in the Scripture that outlines the expectations of the laws of the Kingdom.

The Government Established by God

The first absolute established in the Scripture is the government, as established by God. The government of every nation has been established by God and is literally God's delegated authority on the earth (Titus 3:1 and I Peter 2:13,14). If I incessantly disobey the law of the land, then I am disobeying one of God's major delegated authorities. If I consistently drive 60 miles an hour when the speed limit is 55 miles an hour, then I am in disobedience to God. Conversely, if I consistently submit myself to the law of the land, then in actuality I am obeying God Himself.

The Scripture reinforces this sound doctrine by defining the one who enforces the law as a minister or angel of God who is sent by Him (I Peter 2:13,14). When a police officer enforces the law of the land, he is enforcing God's delegated authority upon the earth.

I cannot expect to have authority in prayer unless I submit myself to God's delegated authority, which is the law of the land. Every time Christians "pad" or "fudge" on their income tax, they are disobeying the law of the land and will not have God-given authority in prayer. Every time Christians tell "white lies" on their expense accounts, they are willfully giving up the authority that God has meant for them to have in prayer.

Your Employer—God's Delegated Authority

Your employer is God's delegated authority in your life. When your employer instructs you, he is speaking with the delegated authority of God and your obedience to him becomes your obedience to God (I Peter 2:18 and Titus 2:9,10).

Obedience to an employer goes beyond action and embraces attitude as well. When a believer expresses a rebellious attitude toward an employer, he is expressing a rebellious attitude toward God. Believers can obey with their actions, but disobey with their hearts. It is absolutely essential to come under God's authority, not only in our actions but also in our attitudes.

Elders—God's Delegated Authority

Every believer must recognize that the Elders of the church are also the delegated authority of God (Matthew 10:40 and I Timothy 5:17). Elders can be defined as a pastor or as a leader in the church. Every time a church member "receives," or shows his respect, for an elder of the church, he is in reality showing that same attitude toward God. This submission to the Elder is more than just an act of obedience, but it, too, becomes a heart attitude.

If the church body or deacon board is paying their pastor's salary with reluctance, then they are not receiving the elder as God's delegated authority with their attitudes. This lack of respect will have its end result in the lack of authority in their prayers. If, however, a church receives an elder with hospitality and with proper heart attitude, then the church is literally receiving Christ. This proper attitude will manifest itself in the authority that this church will experience in prayer.

Family Structure

The authority structure that God requires in a Christian home is clearly defined in Scripture. A wife is to submit herself to her husband (Titus 2:5). A husband is to submit himself to his wife (Ephesians 5:21,25). Children are to obey their parents (Colossians 3:20). When this God-given structure is recognized and obeyed, a Christian family will experience marvelous authority in their prayer life.

Authority Begets Authority

Obedience to the Kingdom structure is not a nebulous philosophy. The authority of the Kingdom is not a cultural thing. The authority of the Kingdom relates to the delegated authority created by God. When I am under authority, I have authority. When I place myself in obedience in action and attitude to God's given authority, I have authority in my own life over sin and sickness (Galatians 5).

Several years ago a young man came into my office who was having problems in his Christian life. He was consistently failing in trying to live up to the life-style which he felt God had outlined in Scripture. After hearing an anointed message by the Reverend Jerry Savelle, this young man began to recognize the authority that a believer ought to possess due to the imputed righteousness of Christ. He realized, after hearing Rev. Savelle's message, that he must come under the authority of the church. This young man realized that he had heard from God. He and his wife came into my office a second time. However, this time he came with an answer, rather than a problem. He said that he was ready to submit his life to this church and to the pastor. A remarkable change took place in this young man's life as he began to recognize the delegated authority of God. He immediately began to have authority over his own nature.

Authority in Prayer

As a believer begins to submit to the authority structure of the Kingdom, he will immediately begin to notice a change in his prayer life. When we come under God's delegated authority, we will have God's authority. We will be able to command demons and they will obey. We will command sickness to leave and it will have to submit to God's authority.

This revelation concerning the authority of the believer in prayer has been one of the missing ingredients in the church through the ages. Although there are many in the church who have abused their God-given authority, we must begin, once again, to balance our loss of Apostolic authority. Pastors and leaders must recognize that they have been set in authority by God, to be submitted to by the Body of Christ. Pastors and leaders are but one of the many vehicles into which God has placed His authority, including government, family authority and employer authority, all of whom represent the authority of God on earth today.

As we learn to live in this delegated authority structure, we will experience new authority in our prayer life and in our life of overcoming sin in our daily existence. God grant that we may learn to live under the authority of the Kingdom!

Chapter XIII

The Kingdom And Its Lifestyle

"No true civilization can be expected permanently to continue which is not based on the great principles of Christianity."

— Tyron Edwards

Chapter XIII

THE KINGDOM AND ITS LIFESTYLE

The teachings of Jesus Christ define the Kingdom of God in many different ways. One of the major emphases is that the Kingdom of God is an alternative lifestyle. The lifestyle of the Kingdom, I believe, is based upon five major principles. These principles are: servanthood, purpose, productivity, creativity and prosperity.

Kingdom Citizenship

In order to receive citizenship in the Kingdom of God, one must be born again (John 3). This indicates that one is born into the Kingdom of God. Evangelicals refer to this birth process as the "new birth." Colossians 1 states that we have been translated from the kingdom of darkness into the Kingdom of His dear Son. All who have been born again have automatically been made citizens of the Kingdom of God. They have been translated and transformed. They have been made into a new species of people. These new people are the citizens of this great Kingdom.

The Psalmist David asked himself the question, "Why do the ungodly prosper?" Believers today reiterate David's question, "If, in the Kingdom of God, there is prosperity and blessing, why then do many of the citizens of this world prosper and are seemingly blessed greater than the citizens of the Kingdom?" Perhaps the answer to this question comes in the form of yet another question, "Is it possible that the citizens of the Kingdom do not obey the laws of the Kingdom?"

Many years ago I lived in the Philippines. I observed those who were not citizens, yet were living in the nation. These people, though aliens, were respected business people in that nation. They obeyed all of the laws of the land. Many of them adhered to godly business practices. They paid their taxes. They obeyed all of the immigration laws. In spite of their lack of citizenship, they were enjoying the prosperity of the great nation of the Philippines. Many of these aliens became very wealthy in the Philippine economy.

At the same time I observed the citizens of the Philippines. Some had disobeyed the laws of the land. A few had stolen; others had murdered people. Some had committed crimes against the nation and against society. They had the full rights of citizenship, but were imprisoned in their own nation. Though they had all the rights of citizenship in the natural, they found themselves imprisoned because they had disobeyed the laws of that nation.

Perhaps this is also true in the Kingdom of God. There are those who are aliens in God's Kingdom who obey all of its laws. They are a people who are servants. They embrace honesty as part of their character. They are a people who obey all of the laws of the Kingdom and therefore enjoy the benefits of the Kingdom even though they are not citizens. Conversely, many Christians who have been born into the Kingdom of God have violated some of the laws of the Kingdom. They do not serve others. They are unproductive and uncreative. They wallow through life without goals and have no seeming purpose. Perhaps they will go to heaven at the end of their earthly life, but they have never fully enjoyed the benefits of God's Kingdom and have become prisoners in the Kingdom where previously they had all of its rights.

FIVE LAWS OF THE KINGDOM

The Law of Servanthood

All Kingdoms have thrones. In referring to the throne of the Kingdom, the implication is that Jesus Christ sits upon a physical throne. Jesus sits at the right hand of the Father and someday He will return to the earth to sit on the throne in the City of Jerusalem and rule the earth.

However, I also believe that there is a throne *now*. The Book of Daniel states that God would give the Kingdom to the people. The Scriptures repeatedly refer to believers as a Kingdom of kings and priests. If we could truly recognize our rights in His Kingdom, we would then recognize ourselves as kings in His Kingdom.

The type of king that God is looking for was revealed fully only in Jesus Christ. When the disciples asked him about His Kingdom and requested that one of them sit on the right hand and one of them on the left of the gold chair in Jerusalem, He responded in an amazing way. He took off His robes, placed a towel around His waist and began to wash the feet of His disciples. He then turned to them and repeated a truth he had stated many times before, "...he who is the greatest among you, let him be as the younger, and he who governs as he who serves" (Luke 22:26 NKJ). Greatness in the Kingdom of God was found only in servanthood.

Jesus then defined the system of the Gentiles or the world system. He explained that the world system encourages men to dominate over one another and to take authority over other men. His Kingdom was not to be like that, He taught. He described that in His Kingdom those who would rule would be those like Himself. The greatest were those who were truly free to serve and to be a servant of others.

Therefore, the throne of the Kingdom of God is the throne of servanthood. The world system just doesn't work in this world. Only God's system can work on God's planet. The only way that proper rule can be established is through the role of the servant. The businessperson who is a servant to his clients, his employees, and to his suppliers will be the person who truly succeeds in business. A businessperson will never truly be a success attempting to get a customer, employee or supplier to serve him.

Jesus was right. There is only one way to real leadership upon this planet. The only way to become a leader in the God-sense is to become a servant. This is a law of the Kingdom. Unless one obeys this foundational precept, he will never truly succeed.

Many times the pastor causes the role of the church to be reversed. The Biblical role of the church is that the church would serve the community. Often, the pastor and the church go into the community to reach more converts in order to boast of a larger church budget or membership. This is not the Kingdom way. The community is not meant to serve the church. The divine calling of the church is to serve the community.

We will never live by the laws of the Kingdom of God until we can turn the world system around. The Apostle Paul strongly emphasized, "Let every man seek not his own, but the other man's wealth" (I Corinthians 10:24). There is a throne to the Kingdom of God. The throne of the Kingdom of God is the throne of the servant.

The Law of the Cross

The second law of the Kingdom is the law of the cross. Jesus called His disciples to "take up your cross and follow Me." Jesus was not telling them to take *His* cross. He never indicated that they would die for another man's sin. He never indicated that they would have to go to Golgotha's hill and die for one another. What He did indicate was that each of them had an individual cross. The individual cross of each disciple was not that they would bear sufferings or sickness during their lifetime. It was not the trials that they would experience, but rather, it was their purpose in life.

I am the only person in the world with my unique fingerprints. There is no one else like me. There is no one else like you. Not only did God make us as individuals, but He gave each of us an individual purpose in life. Campus Crusade states that God has a plan for every life. I believe that. I believe that God has a plan for each person reading this very sentence.

God's plan for you is to bring constructive change to the world in which you live. Your purpose is that during your life on earth you will make a difference in the lives of other human beings, as you serve them. Your purpose is your cross and your cross is your purpose.

If we are truly to become Kingdom people, we are to find what God has for us in our lives. We are to recognize the calling that God has upon our lives and then respond to that call. Just as the disciples took up their cross of purpose and responded to His invitation to follow Him, so must we. To fulfill the law of the cross in God's Kingdom, we must take up our individual cross of purpose and follow our servant King.

The Law of Productivity

The third law of the Kingdom is the law of productivity.

Jesus spoke in amazing parables concerning the Kingdom. One of the parables that He spoke of was the parable of the talents. The first man in this parable had one talent and he chose to hide that talent. The second man had two talents and multiplied them into four talents. The third man, who had five talents, multiplied his talents into ten. Jesus blessed the man who had doubled his talents from two to four and also blessed the man who had increased his talents from five to ten. However, to the man who had one talent and never increased that talent nor reproduced it, Jesus took that talent away and gave it to the man who had much.

God demands that His Kingdom people be a productive people. God requires that Kingdom people be not only consumers, but also producers. One of the contradictions in the world system is that it does not reward productivity. The example set forth by the parable of the talents is that productivity and creativity are to be generously rewarded.

In the world system the government taxes the very people who produce its income. The irony in the taxation system is that the government produces nothing except that which the business community produces for them. Perhaps there is no other method in which to govern, but often we deify that which does not produce and belittle that which does produce. The laws of the Kingdom of God require that all are to be productive citizens of the Kingdom. In order to fulfill the law and expectations of the Kingdom, one must be a person who is both a contributor and a producer in the world in which we live.

The Law of Creativity

The fourth law of the Kingdom of God is the law of creativity. The Bible states that Daniel had God-given wisdom to solve difficult problems.

The Apostle Paul in Colossians says that all believers have the exciting privilege of experiencing "...Christ in you, the hope of glory" (Col. 1:27). God-given visions and dreams are among the most exciting realities of our Christian existence. The Scripture states, "In the last days your old men will dream dreams and your young men will see visions, and upon my servants and handmaidens will I pour out my Spirit" (Joel 2:28,29). A significant aspect of the great day of outpouring of the Holy Spirit is the giving of visions and dreams to the children of God.

The scripture accounts that it was a *dream* of Joseph's that brought an answer to the famine in Egypt. In recent world history, it was the dreams and visions of Jonas Salk that birthed the polio vaccine. The dreams and visions of Henry Ford put America on wheels. The dreams of the Wright brothers gave us the ability to go from one continent to the other in a matter of only a few hours. Through the centuries, dreams and visions of men and women have changed the entire fabric and structure of history.

Colossians 2:3 says that in Christ "...are hidden all the treasures of wisdom and knowledge." Colossians 2:9,10 continues that same thought with these words, "For in Him all the fulness of Deity dwells in bodily form, and in Him you have been made complete." In God are all the treasures of wisdom and knowledge. Hidden in God and in His son is all of the creativity required to solve all of the problems of the world. One God-given idea would solve all of the hunger problems of India. One dream, inspired by God, would solve all of the water problems of Africa. A cure to cancer could be discovered by only one dream, motivated by the Spirit of God.

God has provided the Holy Spirit to create a truly creative people out of His Kingdom people. Name any problem and ask the Holy Spirit to give you an idea. Webster defines an "idea" as a concept, a design, a plan, or a purpose for action. God, through you, can do it. The people of God are the ongoing incarnation of God. In the believer dwells the very hope of Jesus Christ. II Peter 1:4 says that we are "partakers of His divine nature."

Just as God placed ideas in the heart of Daniel to solve the problems of Babylon, so can God give a modern-day believer creativity to solve America's problems. Even as God put a dream into the heart of Joseph to solve the problems of Egypt, God can do it again today. God is still placing dreams and visions into the hearts of His people to solve the problems of our society today.

The Law of Prosperity

The law of prosperity is the fifth law of the Kingdom of God. Prosperity is a covenant blessing. It is an extension of the covenant of Abraham. Prosperity is not a "name it and claim it" philosophy of obtaining whatever strikes our fancy. Prosperity is not just an idea that all of God's people will drive Cadillacs or live in exclusive estates. God promised to bless Abraham and his seed. The New Testament book of Galatians states that we are the seed of Abraham, due to our faith. We are linked into Abraham's covenant and are heirs to the legacy that God promised to Abraham. I am a vital part of that Abrahamic covenant and God is obligated to fulfill His part of the covenant, if I fulfill my part.

There is a second facet of prosperity that we sometimes tend to negate. Many of us embrace a philosophy about financial blessings that has its roots in Greek Gnosticism rather than a Judeo-Christian theology. The Greek Gnostics believed that all matter was evil and that all material things had evil nature intrinsically built into them. The writings of Paul to the church at Colossae emphatically deny the teachings of the Gnostics. In the Book of Colossians, Paul states that "All things were created by Him and for Him" (Col. 1:16). Paul believed that all material things were created by God and were, therefore, good. Even God rejoiced in material blessings. In Genesis chapter 1, after each material thing that God created, He exclaimed, "It is good!" The Judeo-Christian theological viewpoint is that matter is *not* evil, but rather that it was created by God and it is, therefore, good.

Greek Asceticism also has strongly influenced our attitudes concerning financial blessings. Greek Asceticism was the outgrowth of Gnosticism. Ascetics simply believe that in the denial of material and physical blessings of the world a more spiritual people would be created. This denial philosophy was not in alignment with Judeo-Christian thought, but was the direct result of Greek thought. This Greek teaching was brought into the church by St. Thomas Aquinas. The teachings of the Gnostics and Ascetics are diametrically opposed to the teachings of Jesus Christ.

Jesus taught in Luke chapter 13 that, if we would seek the Kingdom of God and His righteousness, we would be blessed with material possessions. This blessing includes financial gain. Colossians chapter one indicates that the Kingdom is to a great extent made up of material things. Jesus confirmed that, when He promised that, if we would seek the Kingdom of God, we would receive material blessings. We are, therefore, to assume that the acquisition of and the use of material blessings is not inherently evil.

I Timothy 5:17 states that the elder who teaches is worthy of double honorarium. I Timothy 6:1 states that the slave is to consider his master worthy of the honorarium which he is given. Therefore, in today's society, the employee is to consider his employer worthy of the wage which he receives.

There is a Biblical concept of material blessing. We are not Greeks in our philosophy. We are Judeo-Christian in our theology. The problem with money is not how much or how little we attain, but whether or not we worship it. There are poor people who worship money and there are rich people who do not worship money. It is not how much money we acquire that determines our attitudes, but rather it is whether our money owns us or we own our money.

Scripture teaches that the riches of the ungodly are destined to become the wealth of the righteous. God has an economic system that He wishes to impose on this world for the benefit of the Kingdom of God. If the people of the Kingdom would serve others, would take up their cross of purpose in life, would be productive and creative, the result of that Kingdom lifestyle is that God's people would prosper.

There is a Kingdom lifestyle. This lifestyle will bring prosperity, but more importantly, a Kingdom lifestyle will bring fulfillment. This Kingdom lifestyle is to be embraced now, for His Kingdom is at hand.

EPILOGUE

KINGDOM NOW...BUT NOT YET is not a theological treatise, nor was it intended to be. It is rather the story of a spiritual pilgrimage of a simple servant of God. It is, to this author, a testimony of an encounter with the Lord of the Kingdom, Jesus Christ. It is a mandate to the author as a person, to become a living demonstration of the rule and reign of Christ in a single human being.

This book was never intended to be the development of a "KINGDOM THEOLOGY," and therefore we have purposely avoided making the manuscript a "theological treatise." Conversely, our purposeful intent was to share with you a spiritual odyssey that began with the Holy Spirit speaking into our human spirit a mandate to "study those things which pertain to the Kingdom of God."

Theologically, my hope is that it will evoke more questions than it answers, and in doing so make us all "disciples" who will turn to the Word of God to discover "truth." Therefore, I have not attempted to provide theological "answers" to pressing questions, but rather to raise questions, to which I have not given answers, or perhaps do not have answers myself. After all, the Kingdom of God is still a "mystery" until that day of full revelation which is yet to come. Yet at the same time the Holy Spirit progressively reveals more of the truth of the Kingdom from the Word of God, as we draw closer to the Lord of the Kingdom.

But most of all the real reason for writing of this book has been to "challenge" the reader to make Jesus Christ the "LORD and KING" of your life, and to make our individual lives the living demonstration of the Lordship of Jesus Christ. I am convinced that until the church understands the necessity for making Jesus the absolute monarch of our life, both corporately and individually, we will never fully comprehend what the church is all about.

You may have read to criticize, or you may have read to learn. Whatever your motiviation, I want you to know that the author is only a "learner." I am desperately attempting to discover more of the person of Jesus, and to learn how to make Him the Lord of my life.

Beyond his Lordship in my individual life I have attempted to challenge you as to how his sovereignty in our individual lives will enable us to be the salt, light, and leaven in a dark and sinful world. I want desperately to know how to be a living demonstration of his Lordship to the world in which I live, yet a world where I am a stranger and foreigner. Further, I have attempted to challenge you to make this discovery with me.

Last of all, the more I discover of His present Kingdom, the more I long for HIS COMING KINGDOM! As never before I anxiously await His physical return to this planet, and the event described by the Apostle Paul in his letter to Thessalonica. What a thrill to be "caught up" with the resurrected saints, to meet our Lord in the air, and again return with Him to set up his final rule and reign over the entire planet. The closer I come to His Kingdom, the more I am prompted to say, "EVEN SO, COME QUICKLY LORD JESUS."

Until that great day may we:

GROW CLOSER TO THE LORD OF THE KINGDOM

CROWN THE LORD OF THE KINGDOM THE LORD OF OUR INDIVIDUAL LIVES

BECOME A LIVING DEMONSTRATION OF HIS LORDSHIP IN OUR LIVES TO ALL THE EARTHLY KINGDOMS WHICH SURROUND US

FINALLY, UNTIL THAT DAY WE WILL PRAY, AS OUR LORD TAUGHT US TO PRAY:

THY KINGDOM COME

THY WILL BE DONE

ON EARTH AS IT IS IN HEAVEN

Introduction To Appendix

INTRODUCTION TO APPENDIX

In my Pentecostal heritage, I was brought up to believe that the return of the Jewish people to their homeland, and the setting up of a Jewish state, would be a fulfillment of Biblical prophecy. This return would fulfill the covenant promises of God to His chosen people, Israel. I was thrilled when, in 1948, Israel became a sovereign nation and that what I had heard preached from the pulpit came to fulfillment.

I was further taught that the Jew was not only chosen by God to be given a land, but further ordained by God to have a full restoration of not only their national heritage, but their spiritual heritage. This teaching concerning God's chosen people led me to a belief that Palestine was divinely destined to be returned to God's people, Israel, and that a sovereign Jewish state would be established according to God's covenant with His people. I believe that those who taught me concerning the covenant between God and the Jewish people were Biblically accurate, and I am thrilled today to have lived to see those Biblical prophecies fulfilled in my own lifetime.

However, in a manuscript where one discusses the "presentness of the Kingdom," we must of necessity discuss the role of Israel and the Jewish people in relationship to the "present Kingdom of God." It sometimes has been assumed that only Dispensationalists (who believe that the Kingdom was rejected, and God's offer of his Kingdom will not be introduced again until the Millenial reign) give adequate place to the Jewish people in their theology. This is not true, for many of us who hold to a strong view that the Kingdom is NOW, yet not fully manifest until His return, also believe in a Biblical relationship between the nation of Israel and God's covenant for the land of Palestine.

I have researched the present day Messianic Jewish community, and found very few Messianic Jewish leaders are Dispensationalists. However, although they are not classic Dispensationalists, they unanimously adhere to a strong Biblical position for a restoration of the land to the historic people of God, the Jew. Although I could deal with this subject, I have chosen to ask one of the very qualified Jewish leaders of the Messianic community who is a highly developed theologian to address the subject of the KINGDOM AND ISRAEL. The following position paper by Rev. Daniel Juster, Apostolic Pastor of Beth Messiah located near our nation's capital, will present a strong position for the historic people of God, and their present and future relationship to God's Kingdom, and to their native homeland.

Appendix

The Kingdom And Israel

"As far as the Gospel is concerned, they (Israel) are enemies on your account. But as far as the election is concerned they (Israel) are beloved on account of the Patriarchs. For God's gift and His call (to Israel) are irrevocable."

— Paul the Apostle
In his letter to the Romans

ISRAEL AND THE LAST DAYS

by

Daniel Juster

Apostolic Pastor, Beth Messiah Congregation

Part A

Milliennial Views and Israel

Today we are seeing an amazing rejuvenation of a variety of views on the last days. The more mature theologians are in dialogue on this topic and are seeking to learn from one another. The less mature are sending their barbs of condemnation across theological borders. Charismatics and pentecostals are involved in these battles as well.

However, current views of the last days, all based on various interpretations of Revelation 20, are neither new nor heretical by the standards of their historic acceptance in the context of the Church. But what are these views?

End Days Theologies

First, there is rejuvenated post-millennialism propounded by a wide group of men who range from reformed thinkers such as Rousas Rushdoony and Gary North to the campus revivalist Bob Weiner. The post-millennialist believes in the visible victory of the people of God in every sector of life before Jesus returns. Believers will rule fully before Jesus returns: He comes after the millennium.

Second, there is a-millennialism which is better termed present millennialism. A-millennialists believe that the millennium is symbolic of the spiritual rule of the body of believers today. They do not expect a literal millennial reign of the Messiah on this earth, with earthly people who are born and die during the next age after the Messiah's return. They do not expect that the present reign of the Messiah in the saints will issue in a total victory on this earth before Messiah comes. A-millennialists have tended to spiritualize as symbolic those passages which predict an age of peace on earth. The next age to the a-millennialists is the new heavens and new earth, the age of eternity.

Today's post-millennialists and a-millennialists both speak of the Kingdom being now. To the post-millennialist it means the visible external rule of the believers unto total victory. To the a-millennialists it is manifestations of this rule in this age, but the Kingdom does not come in fullness until Yeshua returns. The Kingdom refers to the rule of Yeshua which is partially present now but comes in fullness in the age to come. Many a-millennialists have not had a place for Israel's future as a national people since predictions about Israel's glorious future are taken as symbolic of the Church.

Third, we have pre-millennialism in which it is believed that Yeshua returns first; then the resurrection of the saved takes place before the establishment of an earthly age of peace. The place of Israel's blessing is usually seen as a part of this age.

However, it is important to distinguish between historic pre-millennialists, who hold a view of the presence of *the Kingdom now* that is similar to a-millennialists, and dispensational pre-millennialists who believe that the Kingdom refers to the millennial age almost exclusively. The dispensational pre-millennialist also buys into a total scheme of a resurrection of the saints before the great tribulation on earth (pre-trib rapture) and a whole understanding of two plans of God, Israel and the Church, law and grace, etc.

Unfortunately, those who argue these issues do not always recognize that all those who believe in the manifestation of the Kingdom rule of Yeshua now in the various realms of life, family, school, art, politics, etc., are not holding the same position. The more limited Kingdom manifestation of historic pre-millennialists and a-millennialists is quite different from the ultimate victory of the post-millennialists.

Furthermore, even though a limited manifestation of the Kingdom can be substantial, the former two views believe that the return of Yeshua *precedes* the experience of ultimate victory.

A second area of concern is that people have tended to tie a significant role for national Israel to dispensational pre-millennialism. The fact is that the passages used to support these different eschatologies (teachings on the last days) are very difficult to interpret.

My own conclusion from these passages is closest to historic pre-millennialism; yet I can not be dogmatic.

On the other hand, there are passages dealing with God's role for national Israel which are clearly non-symbolic passages. Hence every theology must incorporate these passages without doing violence to such clear texts. Let us now look at Romans 11 which is such a clear passage.

God's Role for Israel

In Romans 11 Paul makes this astonishing statement concerning Israel or the majority of the Jewish people, "As far as the gospel is concerned, they are enemies on your account; but as far as the election is concerned, they are beloved on account of the patriarchs, for God's gifts and his call (to Israel) are irrevocable."

This irrevocable gift and call includes the distinct identity of the Jewish followers of Yeshua. It has broad implications for our understandings. The essence of Romans 11 teaches these salient facts:

1. The transgression of our ancestors brought riches to the Gentiles (Romans 11:11). When our leaders failed to accept the apostolic witness to the resurrection, but persecuted the believers, they inadvertently caused the gospel to spread to the Gentiles.

2. Yet, there is a greater fullness to their full acceptance. Their full acceptance will be the catalyst for the resurrection from the dead. "For if their rejection is the reconciliation of the world what will their acceptance be but life from the dead" (Romans 11:15). This parallels Jesus's words to the Jewish leaders, "You will not see me again until you say, Blessed is he that comes in the name of the Lord" (Matthew 23-39).

3. This last point is further established by Paul when he notes that Israel's hardening is temporary and that she as a nation will be reengrafted (Romans 11:24) and all Israel will be saved (Romans 11:26).

4. To not accept the ultimate salvation of Israel will lead to Gentile conceit according to Romans 11:25.

5. Paul is crucially concerned that a part of Israel be saved as a visible testimony. Hence he magnifies the mighty works of God in his ministry. He knows that a part must be saved so as to lead to the salvation of the whole (Romans 11:14,15). This part that is saved is still part of Israel.

6. Paul notes that the mercy of the Gentile believers, as a whole, is absolutely necessary to Israel's receiving mercy (Romans 11:30,31).

7. Lastly, this ultimate salvation takes place after the Gospel of the Kingdom has been preached to the whole world (Matthew 24:14) and the full number of Gentiles has come in (Romans 11:25).

Against all those who profess that witness to Israel is not necessary, we stress that part must be saved to precede the whole, and that Israel will not see Jesus until they believe; *faith precedes sight*. Israel will believe before the age to come.

However one conceives of the age to come (as a literal age of earthly peace or the new heavens and new earth) one must find a place for the nation whose gift and call is irrevocable.

Now since I am a pre-millennialist, I easily can do this. Israel will be saved corporately when her leaders call upon Yeshua. This is not the individual born again experience. However, Israel welcomes the Messiah King as representative of the nations. This brings the resurrection from the dead for those previously saved, and an age of peace on the earth for unresurrected peoples with Israel. As a corporate acceptance this does not issue into translation into spiritual bodies for most Jewish people.

However, the resurrection saints will now rule and reign spiritually through the Messiah. This includes Jew and Gentile saved before the time of Israel's corporate acceptance of Jesus as King. Effecting Israel's corporate salvation will be the last great intercessory victory of the whole Church. In this the Church will have accomplished its pre-resurrection work.

An a-millennialist could hold to most of the same features. However, the return of Jesus in this view will bring the resurrection for all the saved *including the nation of Israel* which would then be born again and reengrafted. The a-millennialist would have to see the leaders' call for Jesus as ushering in the born again experience for the Jewish people leading to their immediate resurrection. He would see the promises to all believers including the Jewish believers (Israel) as fulfilled in the new heaven and the new earth.

Richard Lovelace, the great historian of revival and an a-millennialist stated, "the promises to Israel will be fulfilled in the letter or the better." There is no necessary implication in a-millennialism to discount the continued validity of God's gift and call to Israel, God's use of Israel in the last days, and her salvation as a prelude to the age to come.

Post-millennialism as well can find a place in its scheme for Israel. Perhaps it is that her salvation inaugurates the millennial age and that Jerusalem will be the center of peace and world cooperation before the Messiah comes. Certainly if the Church is to have full victory before the Messiah comes this includes the gift and call of God to Israel and her reengrafting. The gift and call are "irrevocable" for Israel. Israel becomes one with the body of believers while still remaining a nation among the nations in this age. Post-millennialism need not at all imply a loss for the place of Israel in the purposes of God.

The place of Israel in the plan of God transcends the differing viewpoints on the millennium. The role of Israel is assured by clear didactic passages and should not be controversial. The salvation of Israel is the responsibility of the whole Church and is a key to our hope for the age to come. Intercession, effective witness and congregational planting for Jewish people is an important part of God's call to the whole Church of whatever millennial persuasion.

Part B

Bible Interpretation and Millennial Views

As we noted above there is a tremendous move among many Bible believers to emphasize the presence of the Kingdom today. In its most radical form, this teaching reflects a new post-millennialism with similar features to some of our American Puritan ancestors, to Jonathan Blanchard, the founder of Wheaton College, and to the great revivalist Charles Finney. Marcelus Kick's book "Eschatology of Victory" presents a forceful case for this post-millennial view.

Yet when all is said and done, the overwhelming impression of this interpreter is that the Scriptures clearly picture the return of Jesus to be during cataclysmic times. Furthermore, his personal return is a necessary prelude to establishing the age of peace whether understood in terms of the new heavens and new earth as in a-millennialism or as an interim age of peace as in pre-millennialism.

Having to make a choice between pre-millennialists and a-millennialists, I would count myself among the former thinkers.

Some have termed these presence-of-the-Kingdom thinkers as this-worldly and say that they deny the importance of the possible soon appearance of Jesus. This is far from the truth. Kingdom now theology in its moderate form is simply stressing that the Kingdom of God manifests itself whenever people submit to the rule of God. The Kingdom is a synonym for the rule of God. However, it is not just our personal lives or congregational lives over which Jesus has rule. We are people who are involved in every realm of life; the business world, the political world, the world of art, communications, family, etc. If Jesus is truly Lord of our lives we are responsible to demonstrate his Lordship in every sector of life. Hence the Kingdom of God is to be manifest in every realm.

Whenever an area of life is run by Biblical principle or law, the Kingdom is seen. The Gospel of the Kingdom is the Good News of Jesus's rule and He still rules over all. There must be no separation of personal piety from all areas of human existence. The business man must operate his business under the rule of God! We are salt and light. The presence of the Kingdom must be demonstrated in all of life so that God's salvation might go forth and that His judgment might prevail. Kingdom people want to influence all sectors of life! To see charismatic power *conjoined* with this kind of theology is exciting.

Moderate Kingdom People

Moderate Kingdom people predict no total external victory before Jesus comes. Two crucial books form the theological basis for these people. One is "Jesus and the Kingdom" by the late, great historic premillennialist George Ladd, and the other is "The Kingdom of God," by a-millennialist, Herman Ridderbos. Both argue with extraordinary fervor that the Gospel of the Kingdom, or the rule of God now, is the gospel we are to preach.

However, both also produce a strong case that the present manifestation of the Kingdom awaits the return of Jesus and the resurrection. This is the logic of the "already" and "not yet." The Kingdom has come in reality already but has "not yet" come in totality. The future age invades this age; the powers of the age to come manifest now. ("If I by the finger of God cast out demons the Kingdom of God has come upon you" Matthew 11.)

Moderate Kingdom people believe that only by demonstrating the rule of God in all of life, will the battle with the Kingdom of darkness be fully engaged. When that battle rages at its height, Jesus will return to *put us ever*. However, to fight the battle, believers must truly be an alternative Kingdom community.

Optimistic moderates also believe that engaging this battle and spreading the Gospel brings the return of Jesus closer (II Peter 3:10). We are God's instruments being used to further the Kingdom in its present form and that having completed our walk of intercession and total life witness, Jesus will come. This theology among charismatics has ushered in a hope for the unity and spiritual maturity of the Church with a great harvest of souls before Jesus comes. Hence the Church is victorious before Jesus comes even if the world is not totally converted to the point of external peace. The Church succeeds in *achieving* her gospel mission. I must admit my sympathy with these views. And why not?

The Biblical evidence for this thinking presented by Ladd and Ridderbos is strong. Furthermore, it is a theology that gives us a reason to engage all of life. By doing so the Gospel itself is more effectively preached for it has relevance to all of life. Yet, it does not lead to a "pollyanish" hope of somehow winning the whole world to our side. Satan will have his people as well, and many will always turn to evil until Jesus comes, even unto the anti-christ in the last days.

Moderate Kingdom theology does have implications with regard to Israel. I believe that Scripture teaches that one of the great battles to be won is in intercession, and a key to world redemption is the salvation of

Israel. The whole Church is an instrument of this salvation according to Romans 11:30,34.

However, it is important for me to express why I believe that historic pre-millennialism is the best of all the Kingdom theologies as it relates primarily to Israel.

Historic Pre-millennialism and Israel

Paul states in Romans 11:29, that "the gifts and call of God to Israel are irrevocable." This is so even though they, as a majority, are enemies of the Gospel, for they are loved on account of the patriarchs.

To fully understand this, we need to "unpack" the meaning of the phrase "the gifts and call of God to Israel." A study of the Torah and the Prophets alone make this clear. We are all aware of God's past gifts and call to Israel as a witness among the nations. Yet it is clear that Paul in this verse has in mind a future gift and call. Of what does this consist?

It at least includes her preservation and the promise of her ultimate re-engrafting. This is argued even by post-millennialist David Chilton in "Paradise Restored" but is held by some a-millennialists as well. A distinct continued identity after this engrafting is, however, denied.

It is true that Israel's continued preservation as a people is a testimony to the faithfulness of God who promised it absolutely in Leviticus 26:44. According to this verse, despite her sins, though scattered and diminished, God would never make an end of Israel. Yet Paul's words certainly imply more than this.

First, let us note that Israel's unique life-style, so far as it is Bible rooted, constitutes a unique gift and call. Wherever a Jew celebrates the Sabbath, he testifies that God is the Creator of life and the Lord of History. The whole Jewish Biblical calendar is a testimony to God's great acts in history. Even New Testament events are tied to the Jewish calendar. However, these celebrations also point to God's future age to come, the Sabbaths to the millennium and eternity, Tabernacles to the ultimate Kingdom, and Passover to the great ingathering of Israel and all the Saints (Jeremiah 16,23; Numbers 4:16,17; Isaiah 27:12,13). Hence, Jewish Biblical lifestyle, even in the New Covenant age, is a unique witness to many spiritual truths!

Second, Israel has the privilege of inviting Jesus to be Lord of all nations since she is the representative nation among the nations. Hence Matthew 23:37-39 wherein Jesus says that Jerusalem (the Jewish leadership) will not see Him again until they say, "Blessed is He who comes in the name of the Lord." However, when Israel sees Him, that is when all the nations will see and mourn (Matthew 24:30). The Jewish believer in Jesus shares this call.

Israel after the Return of Jesus

Up to this point the a-millennialist can agree. However, the great divide between pre- and a-millennialist is the place of Israel after the return of Jesus. Is there still a special gift and call of God to be fulfilled?

At issue here are numerous Old Testament passages that describe an age of peace on this earth. Features of this age describe a Jewish people returned to their land, a land of peace and prosperity. Furthermore, they describe all the nations being represented at Israel's tabernacle feast (Zechariah 14). This age is inaugurated after the defeat of the nations that have come against Israel. The nations that survive come to the light of God (Zechariah 8:20-23).

The prophets are consistent in describing this age. It is an age of peace under the rule of the Messiah King. It is an age in which the nations do homage to the Jewish people (Zechariah 8:23). It is an age in which people are born and die. Jerusalem stands as capitol of the nations. The passages are too numerous to quote or exposit in this paper, but what are we to make of them?

They fit readily into a pre-millennial scheme. When the Church has completed its task to witness and intercession, the resurrection occurs. Prior to this very moment, Israel, in dire straits, has had sufficient witness to call upon the name of Jesus (Yeshua). This is through her representative leaders. However, Israel is not thereby resurrected bodily. The leaders who call on Jesus welcome him, corporately. This is not yet the born again experience. Hence Israel enters a millennial age with the nations as unresurrected. The saints rule the world spiritually as resurrected or translated beings through Israel primarily, and through other national representatives. Hence in deception, there can still be one last rebellion (Revelations 20) at the end of this rule with a rod of iron. (A rule with a rod of iron seems inappropriate to the eternal age of the new heavens and new earth. Revelation 19:15) I believe that the relationship of the resurrected to those still in natural existence on earth is similar to the relationship of the resurrected Messiah during the forty days between his resurrection and ascension.

An a-millennialist must interpret these passages as symbolic. The return of Jews to Israel is said to be symbolic of the gathering of the Church in the resurrection, the age of peace in which the man who dies at 100 is considered to be cut off in his youth, is looked at as symbolic of the age of eternal life. The prosperity of Israel must be understood as referring to the prosperity of the church.

The a-millennialist looks at the pre-millennialist as having been naive and simplistic in his Biblical interpretation and this interpretation is seen as wooden literalism. He never tires of showing how prophecies of the last days and the age to come are full of symbol and metaphor. This is apocalyptic literature, a literature not intended to be taken literally. How shall I respond?

Symbolic versus Literal Interpretation

It is true that we must take the Bible and interpret it naturally, not always literally. We need to look to the author's intent and the contemporary understanding. Yet the a-millennialist broadens the meaning of apocalyptic to include too much. Not all vision and prophecy of the future is highly charged with symbol and metaphor. Some passages are more literal and simple in reading than others.

Furthermore, the prophet and his audience certainly would have understood prophecies concerning Israel's future to refer to Israel as a national people.

Does this rob the Church of God's promises? No, by her engrafting the Gentile believing wing of the Church receives every Biblical promise that is pertinent to her. The a-millennialist engages in a method of Old Testament interpretation in these passages which is terribly subjective. He believes he has such a warrant because the New Testament so interprets the Old. I believe he is mistaken on this point.

The New Testament applies Old Testament promises for Israel to the Church because of her engrafting. However this is an application of the text by spiritual principle to God's new people of promise but does not provide the primary meaning or interpretation of the Old Testament text. The text must be understood in its original authorial context. We can not defend taking the New Testament in its natural sense while becoming subjective in Old Testament interpretation.

On this issue I have developed what I believe are key principles of interpretation that must be followed to avoid subjectivism. They are as follows:

1. To defend taking a text as symbolic there *must be clear evidence in the text that it is intended to be so taken* and how far it is to be so taken.

2. We must avoid dismissing the natural sense of a text by saying that the biblical people were at a more limited stage of understanding and hence could only understand a higher truth in the limited terms it was delivered in. This type of argument is rampant and disastrous in biblical interpretation.

Israel and the Last Days

There are limited times when this misapplied principle could be true. We first need to realize that biblical people were much more capable in their understanding then we generally give them credit for. I hold that one must not say that God had to express Himself in the limited concepts of their time unless we can make a strong case for why the ancient biblical people could not have understood what is really supposedly meant. Some examples will clarify this.

Often, the a-millennialist will argue that the reason the prophets speak of the age to come in terms of people living a long time before dying is that ancient people could not understand the concept of an everlasting, resurrected life. I have never seen evidence put forth to substantiate this. Ancients were more readily able to understand such things than we more "realistic" moderns. If God meant this to mean everlasting resurrected life, He could have said so and the ancients would have understood. Already they knew of the "Tree of Life" in the garden of Eden. They could have simply been told of an age in which people would never die but would eat of the tree of life. Even the Egyptian book of the dead had eternal life in it.

When an a-millennialist reads passages on the regathering of Israel he understands it to be prophetic of the Church. Since Israel was the only existent Church of the Old Testament it is said this was the Old Testament way of explaining the salvation of the Church. Yet if that is what God meant he could have said so. It was not beyond the people's understanding to be told that in the future all the faithful from many nations who would attach themselves to God would be gathered together in a New Kingdom of peace and righteousness in a new heavens and a new earth.

To a limited degree the argument could be used, but not with regard to the aforesaid spiritual realities. What the ancients could not readily understand is modern technology. What would a vision of a computer mean to the ancients? An airplane — a big bird? Hence the last days wars are described with implements of war which were common, for there are good grounds to believe they could not understand modern technology and weaponry. (This is argued in Milliard Ericson's "Interpreting the Bible.")

3. Although it is proper to see an application of the promises to Israel to the Church it is not proper to see such applications as the true underlying meaning.

For example, Israel is promised the land of Israel. By application the Church receives the promise that "the meek shall inherit the earth."

Israel is promised a national regathering (Isaiah 27). The Church is promised a gathering to the Messiah (I Thessalonians 4:16). Israel is a nation of priests, the Church is a Kingdom of priests too. However, New Testament application does not replace the original intended meaning. Rather, since all the promises of God to those who are in the Messiah Yeshua are "Yea and Amen" (II Corinthians 1:20), all believers have similar and parallel promises as grafted in people but not in such a way as to invalidate the unique gifts and call (or promises of God) to Israel (Romans 11:29).

If these considerations are true, then we can see that a pre-millennial view is a necessary inference from Scripture. It is neither naive nor foolish.

The millennial age is a glorious transitional age which demonstrates the truth of God's principles to the nations of the world and is a great age of salvation. We could say that Israel is used in this age to establish the world-wide millennial Church.

We therefore believe that Paul had the promises of the prophets concerning Israel's millennial glory in mind when he spoke of the gifts and call of God as "irrevocable" (Romans 11:29).

The Jewish believer remains a part of the gifts and call of God to Israel in this age. He will plan a role toward his people as the part of Israel that is saved. The resurrection of the Church as a whole will issue in the age of peace or the world to come.

For the reader who can not receive our pre-millenialism, our hope is that Israel will play a significant role in your understanding of the last days. The role of Israel in world redemption does transcend the three major views we have discussed.

We can, at least, be agreed on the significance of Israel in this age and her role in leading to the age to come even if we are not agreed upon the age to come and its outlines. May the Messiah come soon!

NOTES

[1] Vinson Synan, "Pneuma" (Pasadena, Calif.: The Journal of the Society for Pentecostal Studies," 1984)

[2] A. Meyer Pearlman, "Knowing the Doctrines of the Bible," (Springfield, Mo.: Gospel Publishing House, 1937)

[3] Ralph Riggs, "Dispensational Studies," (Springfield, Mo.: Gospel Publishing House, 1948)

[4] Clarence Larkin, "Dispensational Truths," (Philadelphia, Pa.: Larkin, 1918)

[5] op. cit. (Pearlman)

[6] Ralph M. Riggs, "Path of Prophecy," (Springfield, Mo.: Gospel Publishing House, 1937)

[7] E.S. Williams, "Systematic Theology," (Springfield, Mo.: Gospel Publishing House, 1935)

[8] I. John Hesselink, "On Being Reformed," (Ann Arbor, Mich.: Servant Books, 1983)

[9] Isaac Rottenburg, "The Promise and the Presence - Toward a Theology of the Kingdom of God," (Grand Rapids, Mich.: Eerdman's 1980)

[10] Tommy Reid, "The Exploding Church," (Plainfield, NJ: Logos International, 1979)

[11] A.T. Clawson, "A Bonhoeffer Legacy," subtitled, "Essays in Understanding," quoted from a pamphlet by Douglas C. Bowman, who was quoting a chapter by Harvey Cox, entitled, "Beyond Bonhoeffer? The Future of Religionless Christianity," which was from a book entitled, "The Secular City Debate," edited by Daniel Callahan (New York: Macmillan, 1966)

[12] WE, Widerstand und Ergebung. Briefe und Aufzeichnungen auf der Haft. (Munich: Christian Kaiser Verlag, 1951) LPPE, Letters and Papers from Prison (London: SCM, 1971; New York: Macmillan, 1972)

[13] Jeremy Rifkin, "The Emerging Order," (New York: G.P. Putnam's Sons, 1979)

[14] op. cit. (Rifkin)

[15] Robert E. Webber, "The Secular Saint," (Grand Rapids, Mich.: Zondervan Corp., 1977)

[16] op. cit. (Rifkin)

[17] Pat Robertson, "The Secret Kingdom," (New York: Bantam Books, 1982)

[18] op. cit. (Rifkin)

[19] op. cit. (Webber)

[20] op. cit. (Hesselink)

[21] John Calvin, "Institutes of Christian Religion," 6th American Edition (Philadelphia, PA: Presbyterian Board of Christian Education, 1928)

[22] op. cit. (Hesselink)

[23] ibid. (Hesselink)

[24] This might appear to contradict the Heidelberg Catechism, which affirms that we are "so perverted that we are altogether unable to do good and are prone to do evil." However, the reference in the Heidelberg Catechism, Dr. I. John Hesselink, op. cit., believes refers to moral good.

[25] Douglas C. Bowman, "Bonhoeffer and the Possibility of Judaizing Christianity," from Bowman's "A Bonhoeffer Legacy; Essays in Understanding," edited by A.J. Klassen (Grand Rapids, Mich.: Wm. Eerdmans, 1981)